# Preparing the perfect job application

# Preparing the perfect job application

## Application forms and letters made easy

### 5th edition

## Rebecca Corfield

**KOGAN PAGE**

London and Philadelphia

**Publisher's note**

Every possible effort has been made to ensure that the information contained in this book is accurate at the time of going to press, and the publishers and author cannot accept responsibility for any errors or omissions, however caused. No responsibility for loss or damage occasioned to any person acting, or refraining from action, as a result of the material in this publication can be accepted by the editor, the publisher or the author.

First published as *How You Can Get That Job!* in 1992
Reprinted 1994, 1995
Second edition 1999
Third edition 2003
Fourth edition 2007 published as *Preparing the Perfect Job Application*
Fifth edition 2009

Kogan Page Limited
120 Pentonville Road
London N1 9JN
United Kingdom
www.koganpage.com

Kogan Page US
525 South 4th Street, #241
Philadelphia PA 19147
USA

© Rebecca Corfield 1992, 1999, 2003, 2007, 2009

ISBN  978 0 7494 5653 5

**British Library Cataloguing in Publication Data**

A CIP record for this book is available from the British Library.

**Library of Congress Cataloging-in-Publication Data**

Corfield, Rebecca.
    Preparing the perfect job application : application forms and letters made easy / Rebecca Corfield -- 5th ed.
        p. cm.
    Includes index.
    ISBN 978-0-7494-5653-5
    1. Résumés (Employment) 2. Applications for positions. I. Title.
    HF5383.C653 2009
    650.14'2--dc22
                                    2009017476

Typeset by Jean Cussons Typesetting, Diss, Norfolk
Printed and bound in India by Replika Press Pvt Ltd

# Contents

Look on our website for supporting downloadable job application forms that can be adapted for personal use.

To access, go to
www.koganpage.com/PreparingThePerfectJobApplication
and enter the password: JA4347

# Introduction

## What are application forms?

This book is all about application forms: what they are, their purpose and how to fill them in. It is not a glamorous topic. Nor is it a topic that anyone is keen to learn about but for the fact that often an application form is the first hurdle that has to be cleared to get a job. It is the part of the selection process that is seen as the necessary but unpleasant task – done in a rush, under protest and without enough preparation and thought. We feel burdened by having to do so much work accurately reporting on our education and employment experience, anxious about the right way to fill in the sections of the form and, overall, highly embarrassed about selling ourselves on paper.

I have seen too many people lose out on the chance of a job for which they were highly suitable because they underestimated the importance of the application form. Even if they understand how vital it is, there are several other traps that people fall into, all too regularly, when completing their forms. Often applicants just do not understand the reasons employers ask the questions they do. If you have ever applied for a job and not been called for an interview, it is likely that your application form sold you short of that opportunity. You can change your luck by finding out more.

Application forms are the most common method used by employers to recruit new staff. An application form is a document, filled in by all applicants to put themselves forward for a particular job. It enables the employer to compare and contrast the candidates. In this way a group can be selected to be invited for interview. This process is often called shortlisting: a longer list of applicants is whittled down to a smaller number or a shorter list.

Application forms can be printed pieces of paper that are sent and delivered by the post. They may be any length between two and eight pages. Increasingly they take the form of an electronic document that is completed and sent via e-mail (electronic mail). Organizations' websites can often contain the relevant application form when a vacancy arises, and candidates simply fill it in and return it through the website or by e-mail to the recruiter.

The whole purpose of completing an application form is to impress an employer enough to win yourself a place on the day the interviews take place. You should complete the form after thinking about the position, and you need to try to present your skills and experience in the light of what is required for the job. Often the employer will send out details about the vacancy in the form of a job description and a person specification. A job description is a succinct summary of the main duties and responsibilities of the job, designed to convey to applicants and eventual job-holders the key areas of work. A person specification is an outline of the kind of person that the employer requires for the job. Often a person specification will include both essential attributes for the role and preferred ones.

# Example

---

Position: Finance Manager

## Job description

Main duties:

- Running small, busy finance department
- Organizing payroll and monitoring income and expenditure
- Managing team of three finance staff
- Working closely with Director and providing regular reports for management
- Liaising with other departments
- Sorting out suppliers' or customers' financial queries

## Person specification

### Essential

- Experience of figure work
- Excellent communication skills
- Well organized and able to work on own initiative
- Computer skills

### Preferred

- Management or supervisory experience
- Financial qualifications
- Experience of manufacturing sector

---

The information available to potential applicants can be extensive. The application pack that you download or receive through the post can contain some or all of the following:

- job description – a summary of the duties in the job;

- person specification – an outline of the kind of person required;

- guidance for applicants – an explanation of how to apply for the post;

- company information – details of the organization and its activities;

- application form – the form for applying for the job;

- equal opportunities monitoring form – data for equalities purposes;

- employment status form – concerning your eligibility to work in the country;

- rehabilitation of offenders form – requiring information about past convictions.

Receiving this much information, all written in formal business language, can sometimes seem very intimidating. Just deciphering what all the documents are for can be daunting, let alone knowing where to start on filling in the necessary forms. It is important not to be put off though. You cannot get the job without clearing the first big hurdle of applying for it.

There are three secrets to succeeding at application stage. The first is to take all of the stages of applying separately. When you receive an application pack, reading through all of the information provided, including the forms that you will have to fill in, will mean that you do not get any surprises later.

The second is to complete the forms properly. Doing all your work in rough first means that you will plan out the forms properly. Take a copy of everything before you do anything else and put the originals to one side. If you intend to apply online, print a copy of the document that you will be working on.

The third is to sell yourself. Application forms do not just need the facts about your background. They also have to make you sound interesting enough to get you invited for interview. If you feel doubtful about your achievements and modest about the contribution that you could make in a new job, you have to overcome your reticence in order to create an impressive application form.

## Letters of application

Sometimes an employer asks candidates for a particular vacancy to apply by letter, normally to accompany a curriculum vitae or CV. Such letters of application need to be direct, impressive and clear if they are to enable the applicant to get an interview. They should normally not be longer than two sides of A4 paper. Writing a letter with impact requires you to use good structure for your thoughts, written in punchy language, and provide comprehensive coverage of your skills and the contribution you can make to the organization. It may take several goes to compose the best letter you can, but it could make the difference between success or failure. Chapter 7 contains hints and tips on effective letter writing.

## The importance of application forms

Do you find that you complete application forms as well as you can, but you are not invited to the interview? Something about the way in which you make your application must be holding you back.

Applying for jobs is a complicated procedure. It is also a skill that we are never formally taught and we are rarely able to see examples of other people's efforts. Yet the application form or letter that you send in pursuit of a vacancy is normally the only deciding factor in whether or not you are asked to an interview.

The employer will not have met any of the applicants and so uses the written applications as the sole method of making the critical decision about which candidates to take on to the next stage of the selection process.

Very few people would say that filling in application forms is their favourite pastime. The factual parts about your personal details and background can seem boring to complete and the rest seems difficult because key decisions have to be made about what to include and leave out. The application form stage of the recruitment process is often undervalued. Candidates prepare hugely for interviews, ensure their presentations is first class if they are asked to give one, but assume that if they submit a form it will automatically get them an interview. We leave filling in the form until the last minute, fail to give it the time it deserves and then wonder why we do not get called for an interview. If we have not done ourselves justice it is hardly surprising that we do not make the shortlist.

Application forms need to be given the importance that they deserve in the recruitment process. That means planning the whole piece of work properly and then giving it adequate time and attention. Unless you complete a form to the best of your ability you will not find yourself in the running for any job you want. You need to convince employers that they must meet with you. A well-written form tells the employer that you are a candidate worth interviewing because you are disciplined in your approach, careful in your implementation and that you have a lot to offer.

When times are tough it may take more effort to get the job we want. We have to make our applications more skilful, impressive and with more impact to catch the employer's eye. In some cases we may have to take a longer-term view of our prospects and set our sights a little lower in the shorter term. This can mean taking a job as an interim measure or as a half-way step towards where we want to get to. Certainly giving up is not an option. Applying for jobs more effectively and impressively is a must.

It is vital in a competitive job market to present yourself in the best light. This is not easy but there are ways to improve your techniques so that your application stands out from the rest. All job-seekers can benefit from having well thought-out and presented application forms.

In addition to applying for jobs or for promotion at work, there are often forms to complete before starting college courses or government training schemes. Even if you are in the job of your choice, knowing how to fill in application forms properly is still important. The days of a 'job for life' are long gone and now we are all likely to change jobs many times. This means that everyone needs to be able to impress an employer in writing in order to be offered an interview.

## How to get the most out of this book

This book takes you through the whole process of completing application forms. It starts from the beginning when the application form lands on your doormat, or you locate it online, through to delivering the completed document to the employer. It establishes a system for job applications that enables you to take more control of what happens. Good candidates are not born lucky; they put time, effort and enthusiasm into the task in order to succeed. This book will be especially useful to the first-time job-seeker who wants to know how to stand a good chance of being selected for interview, but even if you have completed many forms before and are a veteran interviewee, it is easy to become sloppy about your paperwork. You may not have applied for a new job for some time and might want to check that you are approaching the task in the best way.

By reading this book, you will be able to check that you are making the most of your skills, experience and personality on every form that you send off. You will come over more effectively to employers and this will enable you to get placed on more interview shortlists. When you are faced with a blank application form, or need to write a letter applying for work, it can be difficult to know where to start, especially if you are not sure what the employer is really looking for. This book takes you through the various stages to help you understand what is going on and shows you what applying for jobs is all about.

Chapter 1 looks at the changing world of work and explains what is involved in the process of applying for jobs. It describes the application form as one method of finding a job and points out the most important aspects of completing it well. Chapter

2 focuses on using the internet. Chapter 3 analyses exactly what employers are looking for when they decide to take on staff. Also included is a clear explanation of what leads to failure with application forms. To improve your chances of success you need to pinpoint the most important aspects of the job from the employers' point of view. Spending time thinking about the job on offer and researching the organization concerned can provide all the answers that you need. In addition, approaching the task feeling as good as you can helps your chances of success. In Chapter 4 a typical application form is examined and each section is studied in turn to explain what sort of information should be included. The way that forms look is as important as the information they contain and aspects of presentation are covered in Chapter 5. This chapter covers every aspect of presenting yourself on paper, from using computers to choices of pen and paper. Some common problems and the solutions to them are covered too.

Chapter 6 runs through examples of difficult or unusual questions frequently found on application forms together with suggested answers. A list of dos and don'ts for completing forms is included in this chapter. Chapter 7 shows how letters of application can be written effectively, detailing what to include and how to express yourself in an impressive manner. Sometimes you might want to send a letter with your application form, and how to do this is shown here. Chapter 8 contains five topical case studies, each showing a common situation concerning application forms. The chapter goes on to give a checklist of steps for approaching the tricky task of filling in job applications and takes you through the process involved. At the end of the book you will find a list of other sources of help.

# The process of applying for jobs

## The changing world of work

Even as recently as 30 years ago, a great many jobs would be filled with a direct approach to an employer, such as a letter, a telephone call or a visit in person, followed by an interview. Now the situation has changed. In the past, you might have stayed in the same position for much of your working life; now you are likely to change jobs frequently – perhaps every few years. This may be because you want to move about or it may be because you are forced to make the change, perhaps due to redundancy or some other reason. There will be many people interested in any one vacancy and the employer has to have a way of deciding which few people to interview for each job. The application process is a convenient way for an employer to compare and contrast different candidates.

This forces you to learn about how to present yourself well in written form. Even if very little writing work is involved in the job you want, you have to get over the hurdle of the application form in order to get an interview. The ability to present your views on paper is an invaluable skill in any field, and goes a long way to impressing an employer. Most people dread having to project themselves and find it doubly hard to do so in writing. When you apply in writing it is difficult to know how you will come across to other people. You do not have the employer sitting opposite you when he or she reads your form to see the reaction to what you have said about yourself. This means you have to spend extra time making sure that every application you complete is positive, well written and clear about what you have to offer.

The following sort of advertisement appears regularly in newspapers, inviting interested candidates to contact the company if they want to know more about the available job.

*Job advertisement*

---

### ADMINISTRATIVE ASSISTANT

Flexible person wanted to help run busy solicitor's office. Clerical experience preferred but training given. Full-time, £24,500 pa.

Application pack available from:

**S & J Matthews**
**Solicitors**
**150 The Grange**
**Kelmsworth**
**Northants**
**Tel: 000–000–0000**
**E-mail: matthews@corfield.com**
**or download from our website www.matthews.co.org.**

Closing date 22/9/2009

---

If, after seeing an advertisement like this, you are interested in applying for the job, you need to contact the employer and ask for an application form and further details. It is increasingly common for employers to make application forms available on their company website. You will also find many employment agencies or recruitment consultants who have all the application details for the jobs that they are trying to fill on their website. This means that you can either complete the forms on-screen or download them to fill them in, before e-mailing or posting them back once completed.

Enclose a stamped addressed envelope for the company to return the application form to you if getting a form by post. When you write or phone, if it is not clear from the advertisement, ask if there is a job description available so that you receive all the relevant paperwork. Make sure that you keep the original details of the advertisement to help you apply in case you are not sent any additional information. If you print out details from a website, make sure you have accessed all the job information available.

# Why do we have application forms?

It is worth spending a little time analysing exactly what the application procedure is all about. When employers advertise for new staff they know that they will attract a wide variety of candidates. They want to find out as much as they can about each applicant in order to assess which one will be the most suitable for the job on offer.

To start this process, candidates are asked to write to the employer, either by sending in their curriculum vitae (CV) with a covering letter of application, or by filling in an application form.

Both these approaches will be covered in this book. Application forms are used because employers need some method of comparing the abilities, experience and personalities of those people who apply. A form which asks each person exactly the same questions means that quick comparisons can be made between different candidates. By comparing like with like to assess the relative strengths and weaknesses of each candidate, employers can be confident that they have made the best choice of whom to interview. Application forms have other benefits for the employer too. They show that you can follow instructions about how to complete the form, summarize facts in writing, present yourself well on paper and write to a brief. This demonstrates that you can stick to the discipline of a restricted area for your writing, sometimes even to a specific word count and that you can get your ideas across vividly to an audience.

The types of forms used by employers vary considerably. They can be any length – from one short page to seven or more pages – and they are usually printed. Some examples are included on pages 130–61. The exact number and type of questions depends on the nature and level of the job concerned. Some smaller organizations have the same form for every job in the company. This can make it difficult to fill in for jobs that require fuller answers. The questions have been set as the same for every job from the Chief Executive to the cleaner!

Students are sometimes asked by employers to complete a special type of form called the Standard Application Form. This is a general form which can be used to apply to different companies where candidates are not expected to have much work experience. It contains no printed details of the post applied for or the company where the vacancy exists – these are filled in by the applicant. Copies can be found in student careers offices at colleges. Do not think that this form is taken less seriously because of its name – to be successful your application must stand out from the crowd, whichever type of form your application is written on.

It is possible to take more control at the application stage of job-hunting. Employers only ask you to complete their forms because they are interested in finding out all about you. However, it is difficult to represent yourself properly when you are relying on just a few sheets of paper. The challenge in applying for jobs is to find ways to make yourself sound interesting enough and with something special to offer, for the employer to want to invite you for an interview. To make yourself appear unmissable, you need to convey that you alone have the background, outlook and skills to make a real difference to the organization or company. The employer needs to think that you would have the perfect personality to fit in with the existing team and that you would bring some really unique aspects to the organization. If the employer can see that you have spent time seriously thinking about the job and how you would tackle it, that you have ideas for developing the work and that you are keen and able to learn and grow in the job, he or she will definitely want to invite you to an interview.

Very few people are keen on application forms. Most of us find them a chore and approach the task with a heavy heart. But they are a necessary part of this process and we have to tackle them to the best of our ability. When the application pack arrives, or we download it from a website, there can be pages of material about the job. Just two documents, the job description and the person specification, may run over many pages on their own, never mind all the other company information that is often included.

Sometimes even able and well-qualified candidates are put off applying for suitable jobs because they are daunted by the prospect of filling in a complicated form for a particular job. Pages of questions which require thought and careful preparation can appear confusing and difficult at first reading. However, it is unusual to find a new job without having to fill in some kind of paperwork, so the more forms you complete, the better your chances of success – as long as you do them well.

Making applications for jobs is a serious matter. Each one needs time and care in order to complete it properly. However, even the most difficult form can be tackled successfully given the proper techniques. It makes sense to establish a system to ensure that you give yourself every possible chance to get the job of your choice. As with any difficult task, splitting the work up into smaller, less daunting parts can be helpful. The more you think about the big task ahead of you, the more demoralized you will feel about having to undertake it. If you just work on one separate part at a time, starting with the factual questions about yourself, you will be able to make a start. Most of this section should be easy to complete. Next come the two sections on your education and the jobs you have had. These may require some thinking to properly reflect your knowledge, experience and skills. The most difficult questions pose the most problems and they are normally left till last. They ask why you want the job, why the employer should choose you and what makes you think you are a suitable candidate. These require fully planned answers, creative thought about the way to put things down and a thorough appraisal of what kind of candidate the employer will be looking for to fill this particular vacancy.

The next few chapters explain in detail how to organize yourself to be successful. In addition to using good techniques, you need to be in the right frame of mind to 'sell yourself' effectively on paper. To establish yourself in the mind of the employer as someone worth interviewing, you must believe it yourself! There is more later, on page 42, about increasing your self-confidence.

The only way to get a job is to keep making applications to different employers. Assuming that you fill in your forms to a high standard and are applying for suitable jobs, you are bound to succeed eventually. It is important to evaluate your progress and learn from your experience of job-hunting, so that you can continually improve your applications. Applying for a series of jobs at the same time not only increases your chances of success but also ensures that you do not build up your hopes around any one job in particular. You will not be so disappointed at rejection for a certain position if you know that you have other applications in the pipeline, any of which could be successful.

However, there is no point in making applications if you are not really serious about the vacancy. Do not just go through the motions of applying. If you do, your efforts will be half-hearted and a rejection is inevitable. Choose to apply for jobs that would motivate you, and put all your efforts into presenting yourself to the best of your ability.

Making an application is an unavoidable part of the process of trying to get a job, so you have to try to come over as well as you can right from the start.

## Points to remember

1. The application part of the job search process is vital if you are to get an interview. It is not just a formality. Your success depends upon how well you do it.

2. Employers need to know all about you in order to decide if they would like to meet you in an interview.

3. By doing some careful planning you can choose the best way to describe yourself on an application form.

4. Many application forms are now submitted online and those sent in hard copy may be scanned by the employer, so legibility is more important than ever.

## Dos and don'ts

✔ Do start each application afresh with enthusiasm and energy.

✔ Do prepare to spend considerable effort on every application you make.

✔ Do allow yourself plenty of time to complete and check the form.

✘ Don't keep all your eggs in one basket – keep applying for different jobs that interest you.

✘ Don't make flippant applications – if you are going to do it, do it properly.

✘ Don't lose track of your applications – be organized about your paperwork.

# 2

# Using the internet

There are many sites on the internet that give you assistance with job search. Most are sites displaying job vacancies. They make their money from recruitment advertising by employers, or by taking a commission from employers if they place you in a job. As part of the information they provide around searching for jobs, these sites often include tips on CVs, completing applications, interview techniques and other career development issues.

Job-seekers can access these pages free of charge, although if you want to use their specialized targeting process for locating the most relevant jobs to suit you, you may be required to go through a registration process. Many sites have an e-mail facility that can let you know regularly about targeted jobs that fit your profile and some will alert you by text message to your mobile phone when an appropriate job comes on their books.

The world wide web is a fast-changing scene, and new sites appear as fast as others fall from view. Here are 10 of the current top sites for UK job-seekers.

## 1 www.timesonline.co.uk

The website of the *Times* newspaper group. This site contains 'Career and Jobs', their job search pages. These are particularly useful for senior, managerial, technical and secretarial vacancies. The site also includes topical interview tips and career development articles.

## 2 www.prospects.ac.uk

Labelled as the UK's official graduate careers website, this site is provided by the Higher Education Careers Services Unit and the Association of Graduate Careers Advisory Services. It is aimed at graduates and provides 'the essential guide to graduate careers and postgraduate study in the UK' according to the home page.

Accessible and functional, this is a useful resource for graduates, and by gathering all the key points together can help to focus graduate job search or the path to further study. There is extensive job search information and advice here.

## 3 www.jobs.guardian.co.uk

'The UK's most popular newspaper website.' Provided by *The Guardian* newspaper group: *The Guardian* is the national newspaper with the largest selection of jobs. This site is accessible and impressive, and is easy to search for jobs by relevance to your needs. It has many new jobs every day, listed by broad sector and seniority, and is worth checking on a regular basis for national-level jobs.

## 4 www.exec-appointments.com

This is the recruitment site provided by the *Financial Times* newspaper. It includes job vacancies, particularly in the financial sector, and some job search tips.

## 5 www.jobs.co.uk

This site is a recruitment portal which can help to find vacancies that may suit you. It links up direct to all the sites it finds for you.

## 6 www.targetjobs.co.uk

Thie site covers graduate jobs and contains job-seeking and applications advice.

## 7 www.reed.co.uk

This extensive site is owned by Reed, a leading employment agency. It includes voluntary opportunities and career tips, including job search techniques under the 'career tools' section. It labels itself 'the UK's biggest job site'.

## 8 www.bradleycvs.co.uk

This is a CV service company offering information about job search skills. This site also has many links to other specific recruitment sites.

## 9 www.monster.co.uk

A commercial recruitment website with extensive job search advice included.

## 10 www.jobsgopublic.com

A public sector and not-for-profit jobs website.

# Applying for jobs online

Many organizations now recruit directly through the internet. They assess application forms and forms that have been filled in on their organization's website, or they work with specialized recruitment websites to search for applicants who might be suitable for their vacancies. It is both cheaper and quicker for companies to accept online applications. They do not have to pay a recruitment agency to select staff for them, and they (and you) can access the applications any time of the day.

Many companies prefer to get applicants to complete application forms rather than invite CVs to be sent in. Application forms can be worded specifically to the requirements of the job, and they allow straightforward and quick comparisons to be made between candidates. When every applicant has had to answer exactly the same questions, it becomes much easier to decide which answer is the best.

Do not be scared of using the internet as a method of applying for jobs. It can be a powerful way of getting yourself in front of an employer, and shows you can handle new technology. For some jobs it is now the main way to apply – in the IT sector for example and with large employers. However, it is worth being aware that there are some differences when applying for a job using electronic application and selection methods.

Applying online may mean that your document appears in a different layout at its destination from the way it looked when you e-mailed it. It may also change again when dealt with, copied or scanned at the employer's premises, and sometimes it also passes through an intermediary such as a recruitment agency. This means that online applications need to be constructed and presented in a way that takes account of how they will be sent, received and processed.

## Downloading the document

There can be more than one way to fill in an application electronically. Often when you visit a company's website you will be offered the option to download the application form to your own computer so that you can fill it in and then either e-mail it or post it back to the employer. When completing a form in this way it is always worthwhile to print out a copy of the form to work on before you fill it in on the screen. Unless you can see the whole document in front of you at once, it is very easy to present the form badly, misunderstand the instructions and make basic spelling and grammatical errors.

The form may get distorted if you put too much in any one box. Online it is easy to stretch the boxes to fit what you want to say in them, but this can be a trap. If you write too much compared with other candidates your form will stand out for the wrong reasons. You need to take a view before you start about how much you should write. Having a copy printed out in front of you makes it easier to form this kind of judgement.

Often the form will ask for your supporting statement (or why you think you would be the best candidate for the job) on extra pages to be submitted with the form. Sometimes the length of statement they want will be specified (eg 'One–two sides of A4 paper' or 'Not more than four sides of extra paper'). Do ensure that you stick to these guidelines as that is what every other candidate will submit.

Spelling is much harder to get right on-screen. No matter how often you check for accuracy and grammar, mistakes easily creep in. Printing your application at each stage for checking will make sure that you stand the best chance of finally putting in a well-presented, sensible and correct application.

The other method of applying asks you to complete the application on-screen directly on the employer's website. Be warned! Once you press the 'Send' or 'Submit' button you cannot get the form back, and whatever it looks like at that point is the way that it will be judged by the recruiter. Only send it in when you are positive you are totally happy with it. In order for your form to be instantly readable by any computer that may receive it, you need to write your document exactly as instructed on the form. If there is any doubt about whether your form will be readable, plain text format is the most common internet format.

## Using keywords

When recruiters search through forms electronically they will do so by looking for keywords in each document. So what are keywords? Recruiters identify certain trigger words that they feel should be covered by candidates who stand a chance of being successful for their vacancy. Keywords tend to be nouns describing the kind of work that applicants have done in their past that will be directly relevant to the job on offer. Examples are:

- Management
- Administration
- Organization
- Supervision

- Leadership
- Teamwork
- Project management
- Business processes.

Alternatively they refer to the name of the position held:

- Manager
- Administrator
- Supervisor

- Company secretary
- Team leader
- Business manager.

Or the name of the specific skill or knowledge required:

- Database management
- Word
- Excel
- PowerPoint

- Health and safety
- Graphics packages
- CAD/CAM
- Accounting software.

You can see how these keywords are similar to the transferable skills required by an employer, just specified by single words that identify the key skills and attributes concerned.

Employers searching by keywords will select for further consideration any form that mentions a critical number of the keywords identified. This could be the main way that the forms are shortlisted for the next stage, and the process is carried out by a computer search, which will take nothing else about your form into consideration. Furthermore, the employer may want certain words to be given a high priority by the successful candidates. For instance, if you leave the fact that you have managed teams to the last paragraph, when answering the question about what you can offer to the job, you may not get selected to be interviewed for a relevant position where managing staff is seen to be a priority task.

Identifying the keywords that may be used for a job that interests you will mean that you have to do some thinking and researching about the job. If it is a type of employment that you are already familiar with, think about the many topical words that get used often, and try to incorporate the most familiar into your answers on the form. If it is a new work area that you are trying to break into, research by reading professional journals, talking to people in the business and closely examining adverts for similar positions to discover the keywords that frequently occur when describing the key tasks and responsibilities in the job.

The biggest clues about which keywords to include in your application are found in the materials provided by the employer. When completing your statement you must use the competency headings of the person specification, also taking into consideration the job description, as these two documents will provide all the words and phrases that are considered to be most important.

As you explain how you fulfil each requirement, you will use the points given on these documents to feed back your own experience, relevant positions that you have held and a description of your skills. As long as you carefully use the key words that the documents communicate to you, in the order of importance that the employer lists them, you will be on the right lines.

## Form banks

Some websites exist just to hold online forms in a databank, which can then be accessed by employers looking for candidates. You may have to pay for this service but it can be an effective way of finding out about new vacancies if you have impressive previous experience and transferable skills. You will often be asked to input a geographical area within which you would be interested in working.

## Security

Think carefully about where and how you post your form online. If it is an open site with easy access by employers, you may find that your current boss sees that you are searching around for a new job. Would this be a problem for you?

### Points to remember

1. Many more employers are using online recruitment to save themselves time and money. It is now the standard way to recruit for jobs in some sectors.

2. It is more work to prepare your details to be accessed online but it could increase your chances of being picked out by an employer.

3. Only attempt to send an online form if you have ensured that it will be an impressive document once received by the employer.

4. You still need to find out all you can about the organization to help you present the most impressive application possible and to make your form stand out from the crowd.

5. Always keep a copy of everything you send off for your own records.

## Dos and don'ts

✔ Do update your form regularly so that if employers only want to see the most recent, yours will be near the top of the pile.

✔ Do always include your full contact details and your e-mail address.

✔ Do spend time getting the correct keywords in your form. Examine carefully all the information you can about the employer and the vacancy concerned. Look too at other details for similar jobs at the right level. Use all the significant nouns that describe the key activities in the job or the characteristics required.

✗ Don't apply for more than one job in one company. It will look as though you are applying indiscriminately because you are desperate.

✗ Don't just sit back and wait after you have applied online. You still need to be conducting other job search activities in case you have no success from this approach.

✗ Don't think that because you are applying online presentation is less important. It is just as important, but different techniques need to be used to make sure you create the best impression.

# Useful sites

Some sites specialise in recruitment, others feature a recruitment page, and company or organization sites may also show vacancies within that organization. Some sites work as an online recruitment agency, allowing you to lodge your details with them using your form. Employers know they can search through the application forms and CVs held online to look for suitable candidates.

Websites change frequently so you need to keep checking which sites are offering the most useful service. These are a few of the current recruitment websites that you may find helpful. The recruitment business is highly competitive so don't limit yourself to applying through just one site. Look at several and sample their services to see which of them suits you best.

## General vacancy sites

www.jobs1.co.uk
www.jobtrack.co.uk
www.peoplebank.co.uk
www.topjobs.co.uk
www.totaljobs.com
www.ukjobs.com

## Company websites

General business directory for looking up companies: www.ukbusinesspark.co.uk
Confederation of British Industry: www.cbi.org.uk
Royal British Legion (ex-servicemen and women) www.rbli.co.uk

## Newspaper and publishers' sites

*Telegraph* www.jobs.telegraph.co.uk
*TES* www.jobs.tes.co.uk
*Evening Standard* (London vacancies) www.londonjobs.co.uk
Summary of local newspapers' jobs:
www.fish4jobs.co.uk/iad/jobs

# 3

# What are employers looking for?

## How jobs are advertised

Jobs can be advertised in a variety of ways. One of the most common ways of hearing about vacancies is through newspapers, although other methods involve advertisements on the internet, in the Jobcentre Plus network or local shops, through word of mouth, on local radio stations, and in professional or specialist journals. Larger employers will maintain details of any vacancy for their organization on their website, and application forms for current jobs can often be downloaded direct without having to contact the employer first. Recruitment organizations and employment agencies also publish job vacancies on the internet. Their websites often contain hundreds of jobs that are updated very regularly. Such websites often include a facility for searching for specific types or levels of vacancy, to help you pinpoint relevant jobs more quickly. You can also elect to be informed of suitable new vacancies on these sites as and when they are posted through e-mail and/or by a message to your mobile phone.

Certain local and national newspapers carry advertisements for jobs in every issue, often with different types of work being advertised on different days. The interested job-seeker is asked to apply in writing with a CV or send off for an application form. Newspapers also have their own websites which carry vacancy information. Refer back to Chapter 2 for details of some of these. Companies will often send out information about their products or services, as well as a description of the job vacancy concerned.

However, many jobs are never advertised at all. Research suggests that approximately 70 per cent of all jobs are filled without being advertised. Sometimes employers wait for potential applicants to contact them. Chapter 7 tells you more about the way to write impressive letters of application to send with your CV or to make general enquiries to ask employers if they have vacancies. Some employers tell their existing staff that there is a vacancy and invite applications by word of mouth. They want their staff to tell friends and family about the job, to find a new employee that way. This is why it is important when you are looking for work, or if you would like to change your job, that you tell people you know to keep their ears open for any vacancies. Letting trusted current or past colleagues, as well as friends and family, know that you might be available for a new job can sometimes provide the key to hearing about suitable positions.

Application forms are one method of giving an employer information about your suitability as a candidate for a particular post. An example is shown on page 130. The form may be any length but is usually between two and four pages. Normally printed in black ink on white paper, it contains a series of questions designed to encourage the applicant to give certain information about him- or herself. Usually each of the questions will be followed by a box in which you can write your answer.

## Why applications fail

There are certain approaches that will definitely put an employer off calling you to interview. They involve the way applications are constructed and written. These are the top 10 reasons selectors give for rejecting written applications:

■  It is unclear exactly how the applicant satisfies each point of the person specification.

■  No concrete examples of skills and experience are offered, just general claims that the applicant will be able to do the job.

■  The applicant's answers are vague or unclear (eg 'I was involved with the move to computerize our records,' which could mean anything from managing the project to making the tea).

■  The applicant does not answer the questions on the form fully or properly, eg the answers are too short or they do not do justice to the applicant's skills and abilities.

■  The form has been filled in too hastily and includes spelling, grammatical and/or layout errors.

■  The applicant has not demonstrated that he or she has fully considered all aspects of the job, eg indicating a dislike of paperwork when it is obvious that this forms a large part of the job.

■  The candidate is half-hearted and does not sell him- or herself properly on the page and so does not show any real enthusiasm for the job.

■  There is too much waffle, even if it is interesting to read, making the answers too long by using ten words when five would do.

■  The applicant writes in pretentious, flowery language to try and impress, instead of using normal speech.

■  Jargon is used to describe the key tasks in the applicant's present role when it has not been properly explained.

Without exception, these are easy traps to fall into. In our eagerness to get the form completed, we neglect to think through how it will be perceived by the employer when it arrives.

Reading this list, you may think it is a difficult task to get your application form in just the right state to impress an employer. The good news is that all of these mistakes that could lose you the chance of an interview can be avoided through adequate preparation about your selling points, paying careful attention to the form and the job information supplied and allowing plenty of time for its completion. All of these bullet points will be covered in later chapters so that you can be sure you will not fall into these traps yourself.

## The need to 'sell yourself'

We have seen that application forms need to contain positive statements about yourself. It is not enough to give a list of what you have done and the skills that you have acquired. You need to see application forms principally as a method for you to 'sell yourself' to an employer. In today's competitive job market, there will be many hopeful applicants for every job. Only the most distinctive application forms will stand out enough for the senders to be picked for interview.

It used to be the case that anyone who could satisfy the minimum conditions laid down in the job description would automatically be shortlisted for interview. Although it is true to say that applicants will not be picked for interview without establishing that they fulfil the basic conditions, because of the increasing number of candidates it is now essential to put forward a much stronger application.

Out of 100 applicants for a position, half may be weeded out as unsuitable at an early stage because they fail to demonstrate that they meet the essential requirements. However, this still leaves a large number of applicants who might be able to do the job. The employer will be looking closely for any clues that one applicant rather than another should be taken forward to the next stage. This means convincing the employer that there would be some extra benefit or added value in including you in the shortlist for interview. More applicants mean that the criteria for each job are raised and employers can afford to be more choosy. In other words, you have to try harder and do better in order to succeed.

Jobs are offered because employers need extra pairs of hands. No employer would just take on the first person who asks. Employers are looking for applicants who come trained, experienced and skilled in the work required. The perfect candidate will not only be able to jump right in with little or no additional training but will bring new skills and ideas to the job as a result of his or her previous experience. In addition, the person will be a joy to work with, an asset to the team and endlessly keen and highly motivated. In the real world, it is not often that perfect candidates of this sort present themselves for a job, but every employer is trying to get as close as possible to this ideal. One way employers assess suitability is to look for the transferable skills of any applicants.

All employers are keen to know what skills you have learnt in previous jobs that will be useful in the future. These 'transferable skills' are those that will be helpful across different roles, eg communication skills, computer ability or being a good team player. You need to prove that you are the most 'employable' candidate available. The job description will tell you what specific skills the employer is looking for. Either you have already developed these skills or you have experience that will mean you can easily adapt to what is required and become productive. If you have similar but different experience that means you are confident about your abilities to do the job, you must explain what you have done before and how it relates to this particular role.

Companies are looking for the best candidates for their vacancies and your application needs to shout out loud that you are one of those candidates. But judgement about who is the best candidate will vary according to the job on offer. That is why it is essential to get inside the head of the employer to examine what exactly he or she is looking for with each vacancy. One way to impress people is to show enthusiasm. You are in competition with many other keen applicants who are all trying to impress. A genuine interest and excitement about the work involved in the job shows even through a written page.

Consider the following two examples in answer to the question:

## 'Why do you think that you are suitable for this position?'

(working as an accounts assistant)

*John's answer:* 'I am quite good with numbers. My last job involved calculating and checking figures and I tried to be accurate. I took my GCSE in mathematics and did well at school in this subject.'

*Michelle's answer:* 'Working with numbers is a challenge which needs good attention to detail and special care to be taken when doing calculations. I take a great pride in being accurate and did especially well in the mathematics GCSE course at school. I very much enjoyed my last job which involved a great deal of figure work, calculating totals and checking figures for the department I worked in. Clear communication with clients and internal colleagues was an important part of the role. I am keen to make my career in this area.'

You can see how Michelle's reply abounds with energy and enthusiasm for the work. She achieves this effect by choosing bolder and more definite language, letting the words depict her keen attitude to this kind of work and broadening her answer to include mention of more relevant skills which will be applicable to the job on offer. She creates the feeling that she would come in to work each Monday morning beaming with delight at the prospect of a new week!

# How to approach the task

Application forms are split up into different sections and each is concerned with a different subject. Their sole purpose is to find out about the candidates, and those candidates whose forms contain the most impressive information will be invited for interview. However, it is extremely difficult to put yourself across effectively on paper alone. To create a good impression you need to give the employer as *full details* as possible about yourself. Applicants who do not write much are doing themselves out of their best chance of getting the job. A lot of people write too little, giving too few examples and not enough evidence of their skills.

The most important point to remember is that *neatness* gives you a great advantage in the hunt for the job of your choice. It has been shown that employers will reject perfectly well-qualified, suitable candidates if they send in badly presented applications. There are two reasons for this. The first is that how a document looks creates a strong first impression. The only information that the employer has to go on to decide whether to pick you for interview is your application form. He or she will make judgements about your attitude to work and to other people on the strength of the way you have filled in your form. If you have been careless in your completion of the form and hasty in the way that you have filled it in, certain inferences will be drawn. It will look as though you prepare badly in everything you do, you will seem slapdash and prone to making errors and, as a result, it will be difficult for any employer to think of you as someone worth employing. In other words, you will have ruined your chances before the form is even fully considered if it seems off-putting in the way it has been presented. You need to take a lot of care over how you are supposed to be completing the form, your spelling and how the form is presented physically – the layout on screen if you are e-mailing or uploading it, or the quality and typing on the page if you are posting it. The second reason is that it is hard to take in information from the printed page, let alone the handwritten one, and neat writing is much easier to follow than messy scrawl. Your application form needs to be as well presented as possible to stand out from the rest without being distracting. Chapter 5 gives more tips on how to ensure all your application forms are well presented.

Sometimes it is tempting to send in your CV instead of spending time filling in the same information on the form. However, if the employer wanted your CV, he or she would have asked for it. To send it as a substitute for filling in an application form tells the employer that you cannot really be bothered to spend time applying for the job. It also shows that you are not prepared to follow instructions. Of course, if the company asks to see your CV in addition to your application form that is quite a different matter. In this case the CV should be short and concise. More than two or three pages will be too long to hold the reader's interest. But when you are answering the questions on the application form you need to make your answers long enough to interest the employer without being long-winded.

You have to comply with all the instructions given on the form. If it tells you to complete the questions in a certain way – do it exactly that way – for instance, using a certain colour of ink or capital letters. The instructions will be there for a good reason, even if it is not clear to you.

Beware too of simply copying information from one job application to the next. Each and every new application form needs to be treated as though you are starting anew. Of course, the factual details about your background will be the same on each one but the way you present yourself should be specifically tailored to the job in question.

The well-written response that drags on is liable to bore the reader just as much as the poorly written one. To make sure that your answers are written in a coherent way, you must *organize* your thoughts in advance. Chapter 4 gives more information about thinking through and planning your answers systematically before you start to write anything. This ensures that you do not duplicate, muddle up or miss out any information.

Written applications are, in themselves, an exercise in using discipline, making an effort, sticking to the instructions and showing your writing ability – all of which are very useful in any job.

## Positive mental attitude

Employers are looking for more than just the right kind of answers in the boxes on an application form. They are also looking for people who consider themselves to be winners and successful operators in their field. This may seem a hard attitude to strike if you have just been made redundant, have left your last job under a cloud or have been unemployed for some time, but it will be even more important to create the right impression in these cases. You need to boost your feelings about the contribution you could make, for the very good reason that unless you believe it yourself, you will be unable to convince anyone else of the fact.

There are certain attitudes in job-seekers that will definitely put an employer off. In order of significance they are:

1.  Disruptive, wanting to cause trouble.

2.  Lazy, just wanting to do the minimum possible.

3.  Lack of confidence in own abilities.

4.  Bitterness about previous experiences.

5.  Cynicism about employers' motives.

Do any of these five points apply to you? Have you had bad experiences in work? Do you feel bruised at the current position you find yourself in? Are you down or depressed about your prospects and feeling hopeless? Are you resentful about having to apply for jobs? Any of these feelings will adversely affect the way that you apply for jobs. Our attitude comes over through the way we think, write and present ourselves. Pessimism, surliness or anger will make themselves shown in your application form and do you no favours.

If you feel you may exhibit any of the above you will have to work doubly hard to retrain yourself to come across differently. While it may be totally justifiable to feel aggrieved at the treatment you had in previous work situations, it is not helpful to extend that feeling into the next job. You need to spend some time generating positive feelings of optimism and hope for what could occur.

How do you make your outlook positive and get motivated? You will need to use every good thing in your life to help you. Start by asking those who love you best to tell you what they value most about you. Read old letters or references to see what people find impressive about you. Stick to your normal routines when embarking on a job search programme, as making applications involves uncertainty and risk, and a regular living pattern will help to balance this.

If there are some activities that you love such as having foam-filled baths, participating in certain sports or pastimes, taking weekend breaks or having breakfast in bed, then do them. If you find the company of certain people helpful and stimulating, then invite them round and spend more time with them. Physical exercise can make you fitter whilst providing you with a regular burst of positive energy. Working for other people on a voluntary basis can get you more externally rather than internally focused.

Consider all the times that you have succeeded at something, and try to recreate both the power you put into making the effort and the feeling you experienced afterwards. You need to concentrate your mind on approaching the task of applying for a job in a focused and determined manner in order to do your best.

Getting yourself into the right frame of mind is an extremely significant part of job applications. You are trying to convince employers of your worth and ability just by writing details on a form. It is hard to do this in good times and even more so when you are not at your best. To counteract this, treat yourself especially well. Nurture and care for yourself in every way you can while you are in this job search phase and you will find that it has a positive effect on the quality of your applications. By boosting yourself, you will increase your chances of success.

## Points to remember

1. The frame of mind in which you start making applications can make all the difference.

2. Employers only have the information on the application form to make their decisions about which candidates to invite for interview.

3. Selling yourself depends on strong statements, enthusiastic language and clarity about what you have to offer.

4. Some companies now vet applicants by telephone before sending out application forms.

## Dos and don'ts

✔ Do give priority to making yourself feel good, so that you can convey an impression of confidence to an employer.

✔ Do think about jobs from the employers' point of view, and consider what will have the most impact on them.

✔ Do approach every application sincerely: if it is worth completing it is worth completing properly.

✗ Don't worry about being boastful – all the other applicants will be highlighting their strong points.

✗ Don't waste time applying for jobs that do not motivate you – it will show in your lacklustre answers.

✗ Don't take short cuts to filling in the form; you need to give it time and energy for an application to be successful.

# What to put in your application

The secret of filling in application forms is to take the task seriously. If you are not prepared to devote a certain amount of time to this activity, you are probably not that interested in the job itself. Getting the job you want is an important business and demands the same care and time that you would devote to any serious piece of work such as a college module or a school project.

If you are not keen enough to allow sufficient time for completing the form your application may appear slapdash, without the depth of those of the other applicants. The employer will realise this and you will not get the job. My rule of thumb is that you should aim to spend at least one day of preparation for each page of the application form. Of course, not all sections of the form will take as long as others, and you will not be spending the whole of each day poring over pieces of paper, but this is a rough guide to how much input each job application requires. You may feel that this is a lot of exertion for each job, but think about what you have to gain. The salary (or wages) that you would earn just in the first year amounts to thousands of pounds, which is a lot of money, and is surely worth the investment of some effort. So, given that this is a task which you agree should be taken seriously, what is the right way to complete it? The best way to approach filling in the form is to split the task up into easy stages.

# The planning stage
## The task

When the application form arrives on your doormat, take a photocopy of it. Libraries, job clubs and local shops now have photocopying equipment, although you may have to pay for your copies. If you do not have access to a photocopier, write out the questions by hand on to plain paper, then put the original form away for safe keeping. If you are applying online, print out a copy to use as your draft version. You will now only be working on this copy until you are confident that you have sorted out exactly what to say for each of your answers. In this way you will keep the original top copy in perfect condition until the time comes to complete it.

The secret of a good application is to allow yourself plenty of time before the closing date – preferably a day for each page of the form. You will be undertaking a major piece of creative work requiring effort and inspiration. Impressive writing cannot be done when you are feeling pressurised, flustered and rushed. You need to have an appropriate location in which to undertake this work. Find a quiet place where you can concentrate on the task in hand. You will need a clear desk or table with enough space to spread out all the relevant pieces of paper and a good light by which to read, write or type. Try to make sure that you will not be disturbed, and switch the television off! Give yourself a reasonable deadline when you will cease work – and then get started. Now is the time to concentrate on this task alone, in order to immerse yourself in all the details of the job. Have a current copy of your CV to hand to give you the facts and dates about your career history. Your favourite type of music played quietly in the background may help to put you in the right mood. Focus on what you are doing and try to blank out any other concerns you have or distractions around you. Tell family, flatmates and friends that you are going to be busy and ask them not to disturb you.

## The vacancy

Before you start, re-read the details of the job carefully from any information you have been sent or have discovered yourself. Take a note of or underline the main requirements/ skills/qualifications asked for. If you do not have any of these requirements it is unlikely that you will be asked to an interview. However, if you have different skills and experience or alternative qualifications to those specified and feel that you could do the job, go ahead and apply.

If you can show that your different experience has given you significant other skills that could be relevant to this job, that is, transferable skills, then you could be in with a chance. For instance, if the details about the job asked for staff management experience, which you do not have, it is not necessarily the end of your hopes. If you have been bringing up children and perhaps helped run a community venture, such as a nursery where you organized team rotas and supervised the work of other helpers, this could provide you with skills that would be directly transferable to the role in the job you are applying for.

Many people get good jobs by taking chances like this, on the basis that they do not have anything to lose. However, the onus is on you to state clearly what you *are* offering as an alternative to the qualifications or experience asked for and why your background makes you suitable for the position.

A certain amount of time must be spent thinking through the nature of the vacancy for which you are applying. Each job is different and requires different qualities, skills and experience. Moreover, every organization has a different feeling or culture and is looking for people who will fit in. The big, bustling, high-street department store will be looking for candidates who can work happily in that environment, who enjoy frequent changes, high pressure and large teams. A small country firm of solicitors will require a different type of staff, those who like the quiet atmosphere and settled routines of such a company.

## Yourself

At the planning stage you also need to spend time thinking in some depth about who you are and what you have to offer relative to the company and its requirements. You should prepare a good CV which gives details about your qualifications and experience to date. This can be used as an aide-memoire, or memory-jogger, to fill in certain parts of your application form and also as a confidence booster at a time when you need to be thinking about your achievements. A properly written CV can give an overview of your strengths and skills and help you to present yourself well when applying for jobs. It is vital to link your skills, knowledge and experience to the duties involved in the job.

Now is the time to inflate your own self-confidence as much as possible. On most application forms there is a question about your personal qualities and how these will enable you to contribute to the post on offer. The following exercise will help you to prepare your answer to this type of question. Most of us could reel off a long list of our faults but we find our strengths more difficult to pinpoint. For this exercise, you will need to dispense with the feeling that you are boasting, take a deep breath and describe yourself in the best possible light.

## Exercise: Your good points

Most people find this exercise tricky because we are not used to applauding ourselves in this way, which is exactly why it is such a useful thing to do. Perhaps you can remember being complimented on some facet of your character or behaviour, either in person or in a school or college report. You may have had favourable comments made about you in an appraisal or performance review from a previous workplace. What was said then? How would your best friend describe your good points to someone who had not met you before?

In the space on page 44 make a list of 10 of your good qualities. Each point should comprise one word or short phrase and relate to your behaviour at work, at your best. Here are some examples. You may find some which apply to you and could be included in your list:

| | |
|---|---|
| flexible | articulate |
| calm | organized |
| punctual | tactful |
| sensible | alert |
| quick to learn | reliable |
| practical | cooperative |
| polite | loyal |
| lively | responsible |
| dedicated | versatile |
| creative | good at keeping to deadlines |
| confident | able to work under pressure |
| approachable | hardworking |
| assertive | capable |
| accurate | thorough |
| perceptive | able to work alone |
| consistent | good team member |
| innovative | committed |
| careful | good at managing others |
| strong | competent |
| direct | humorous |
| adaptable | decisive |
| bright | enthusiastic |
| thoughtful | cautious |
| imaginative | patient |
| dependable | dynamic |
| friendly | methodical |
| outgoing | self-motivated |
| serious-minded | sensitive |
| quick | honest |
| buoyant | cohesive |

Everybody's list will be different according to the personality of the writer, so don't feel you have to choose all or any of your words from the examples above. Write your description of yourself here, choosing 10 words or phrases that you feel best depict your character strengths:

1 _____

2 _____

3 _____

4 _____

5 _____

6 _____

7 _____

8 _____

9 _____

10 _____

This type of list is useful for two reasons. First, it provides you with the raw material to answer questions about your strengths or personal qualities, which usually crop up in any written application, and second, it enables you to see your good points laid out on paper as a boost to your confidence. If you are an appropriate candidate for a job vacancy, you of all people need to feel confident that you have the personality and experience to do the job well. Unless you believe it, you will not be able to convey that impression to anyone who reads your application form. So spend some time thinking about yourself, what you have been praised for in the past and the advantages to an employer in taking you on. You will need to have specific words which apply to you that you can use on application forms.

## Your experience

You also need to plan which aspects of your past to mention. Large gaps in your career history will be noticed, but this still leaves you with a certain amount of leeway about how you tell the story of your experience to date. Generally, information provided by you must be relevant to the job (and so will change with the different positions that you apply for) and should have purpose. Otherwise, the good points that you include will be lost in general trivia that does not add anything to your form. The way that information is put over has an impact on the way it is received. It will never be relevant to divulge that you failed a flute exam, but it may be worth saying that you studied the instrument when you were younger.

Active verbs or power words can be useful in describing your achievements to date. The following list may prove helpful when you are writing about your experience. There are many other words which may apply to you but here are some examples:

coordinating
computing
caring
persuading
establishing
serving
travelling
diagnosing
assessing
analysing
copying
negotiating
managing
training
teaching
memorizing
deciding
checking

inputting
growing
advising
recruiting
performing
leading
developing
filing
sorting
typing
loading
handling
communicating
researching
selling
inventing
recording
stocking

| | |
|---|---|
| compiling | delivering |
| carrying | playing |
| helping | working |
| mending | making |
| problem solving | monitoring |
| evaluating | interpreting |
| writing | selecting |
| reading | translating |
| cleaning | supervising |
| driving | planning |
| drawing | enabling |
| liaising | changing |

If you are applying for a certain type of work, the organization concerned will want to see evidence of your direct experience in this field. This means you need to prepare clear examples in advance that illustrate each of your statements.

A national organization which recruits volunteers to work abroad always asks candidates if they have done any voluntary work before. Applicants often answer 'No' when it should be obvious that this will not be sufficient and will place them at a disadvantage. In such a case the employer needs to be convinced that you are capable of sustaining an interest in volunteering. Even if the experience was some time ago it is worth mentioning. Candidates for this type of vacancy with no voluntary experience should join a scheme and get involved in some voluntary work immediately so that they can fill in the form adequately. If they have not picked up some experience of this key area of the job, their application is likely to be rejected at an early stage.

## Analysing the job

Deciding what skills and abilities are required is not a matter of guesswork but of using common sense. Consider the following job advertisement:

---

### TREETOPS NURSERY

Small estate-based nursery needs a part-time childcare assistant to help with general duties. 17.5 hours per week. Personality more important than experience. Training given.

For application form write to:

**Treetops Nursery**
Garrick Estate,
Tonbridge, Kent
or phone 000-0000.

---

Even with these few details we can work out what sort of person would be suitable for the job. We know that the employer is interested in three main things: experience, skills and personality (that is, what you have done, what you know and the kind of person you are). Let us consider each of these in turn.

## Experience

Although the advertisement says that training will be given and experience is not necessary, many applicants will be able to provide some experience, so it would be helpful to provide some evidence of your ability to do this type of work. You may have worked in a childcare setting and have direct experience to offer. Perhaps you have brought up children of your own, helped out in other childcare schemes or been a babysitter or a childminder in the past. Even if none of these examples would be classed as a 'proper' job, this kind of experience would indicate your ability in this area.

## Skills

In this sort of work the right person will be punctual and good at time management. Budgeting and organizing skills will come in handy as well as attention to detail and the ability to schedule events. Knowledge of home economics would be an asset. An awareness of health and safety is important when working with young children and even confidence with shopping would be a selling point. Being able to handle paperwork competently would be a definite advantage. Any experience of close working with other people in teams would be helpful.

## Personality

In terms of personality, we have to think about the sort of person who can work with children. He or she needs to be well balanced, reliable and organized, with a tolerant and happy disposition. Someone who is observant and patient, who enjoys playing with and entertaining children of all ages, and who has an understanding of the problems and concerns affecting children would be ideal. The right person should enjoy teaching and communicating with other people and using his or her imagination. A good childcare worker finds it easy to care for children and is able to create a disciplined environment with the right mixture of fun, learning and control.

These points are the basic requirements for anybody who wants to work with children. To apply for this job, an applicant needs to show that he or she has this type of experience, together with the skills and personality required, by quoting examples from previous jobs.

Any job can be analysed in this way, even with little information to start with. You need to use your imagination, your common sense and research into what is involved in the job. The more comprehensive the information you provide, the more likely you are to be selected for interview. Don't make the employer work hard to dig out the experience you have had that equips you for this job. He or she will not have the time or the inclination to delve deeply into your work background and personality to see if you fit the vacancy. If you do not make it crystal clear from your application that you have a lot to contribute, you will probably get rejected. There is a job on offer and you would like to get it. That means that you have to lay everything out on a plate to make it easy for the employer to see how good you are. That is the only way of progressing in your campaign to get offered a job that you want.

## Finding out more

If you are not sure what the company is looking for, you need to do some detective work. Research into the products or services sold or provided, the numbers of offices or outlets and staff, the main markets and the style of the organization, is never wasted. It enables you to feel confident about your knowledge of the business, and you can impress the interviewer by talking up in the interview about your research on the company.

You can try to talk to people who work at the firm by ringing up and asking for information; you can look up facts about different organizations in libraries or ask people who work in similar jobs for their impressions of the company or the type of work that you are interested in. Companies often advertise their products or services in magazines and local and national newspapers and most now have a presence on the internet from which a great deal can be learnt.

Most organizations have a website from which you can research almost anything you need to know about the company. Often the site will show how the organization describes itself, clearly outlining its vision and mission statement, its outlook and values. It may well include profiles of key staff together with a brief history of, and background to, the development of the company. You may find that the way the information is written and displayed tells you more about the kind of organization it is and how it sees itself than does the content of the site. It may be trying to portray a young, dynamic and creative image, or instead be labouring its pedigree, long traditions and solid trading background.

These impressions are very important, as they can tell you whether or not you would fit well into the organization. Do the

What the employer is looking for

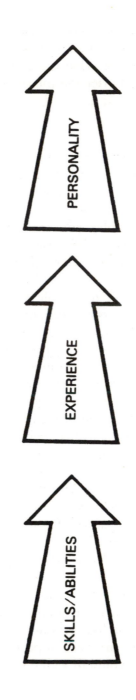

values that the company express seem important to you? Is this the kind of organization that you want to be associated with? Could you see yourself working here? Try to pinpoint exactly what impresses you, so that you can reflect this in your application later on. Not just having done research but being able to show you have done so can enhance your chances of being called for interview.

If you need to locate businesses of a certain type or a particular company, you could use a search engine: a website that can help you track down the kind of information you need. Google (www.google.co.uk) is a useful web resource that can effectively link you to a host of other sites. Researching around the organization that interests you is always worth doing. You may well discover relevant facts about the sector or area of business that could be mentioned in an interview to show your understanding of the kind of work. Make sure that you establish both the good and bad points of the job, so you are confident that you have a realistic picture of both its opportunities and its difficulties.

You may be applying for a different job or a promotion in the organization in which you already work. Do not make any assumptions about being known or about your reputation if you are applying as an internal candidate. This is a really important point which trips up many candidates. Even if you have worked in the same team for years and your supervisor is doing the recruitment for the new position, you must treat the application form as though no one reading your details will have ever heard of you before. You may be working in the department where the new job is located but your suitability for the post will be judged solely on the form you submit and only on the information it contains compared to those of the other applicants. The selection of candidates may be done by a new member of the human resources department who has never met you.

# The preparation stage

## Taking care

First, read carefully through the copy that you have made of your form. Then work your way through it, considering how you are going to approach filling it in. If it is in hard copy, never start writing on the original form straight away, even if it appears easy to complete. Errors and corrections do not enhance any form. If you do not read through a form thoroughly before you start to complete it, you can often make unnecessary mistakes. Some forms have duplicate questions that mean you may only need to complete half the form depending on your situation. If you rush to start writing, you may find that you have filled in a section that does not apply to you.

That sort of error can leave you looking at a messed-up form and feeling demoralized when you badly need more confidence, not less. Sometimes there will be similar sounding questions which require quite different answers, and it is worth checking what the form is looking for in each answer so you can prepare carefully to select the best information to include for each. If you rush to write things down too quickly it can mean that you miss the subtleties of the question, duplicate your answers, and perhaps miss the point of a particular question entirely. If you are not totally confident about your spelling, make sure you use a dictionary. There is no excuse for misspelled words. Line up a friend, relative or work colleague who is willing to check your work later on. When completing an application form in hard copy, use black ink or ball-point pen and not pencils, crayons or felt-tipped pens.

Normally, if the form is in hard copy, you need to make your answers fit the space provided, and fill up that space completely. However, if the form suggests that you may like to continue on a separate sheet of paper if you do not have enough room for your answer, you should do so. The employer is saying that he or she expects a longer answer than there is room for on the page. Everybody else who applies for the job will use an extra sheet and, to do your answer justice, you need to do the same.

Take all questions on the form at face value, answer them directly and never assume that the employer is trying to catch you out. The reason you have been asked to fill in an application form is to find out more about you and see if you are a suitable candidate for interview. However, there may well be searching or difficult questions which will require you to think hard about the job and work out what kind of special contribution you think you could bring to it. There will not be trick questions or ones deliberately designed to confuse or fool you on application forms.

## Completing the different sections

Application forms usually come in two distinct parts, sometimes characterized as the 'easy' bit and the 'difficult' bit. The easy bit is the first section that asks for details about you, the applicant. This normally includes personal details, academic qualifications, work experience, interests and references. This part of the form is often considered simpler to complete because the information is factual to a large extent, and you just need to fill in the boxes with straightforward information about yourself.

Although the information required may be relatively easy to fill in, do be sure that you read the form carefully so that you know what is wanted. If the employer asks for specific information, or requests that you give the information in a particular way, and you do not do this, you may lose the chance of the job. Even if the instructions make no sense to you, it is wise to comply with them. For instance in the employment history section, if the small print on the form asks for your most recent job first and you give the list in date order with your first job at the top, you might stand out as the only candidate who was unable to follow the written instructions on the form, which is bound to create a poor impression. Although this is not a terrible crime in itself, if an employer has 60 applications for one post, any reason to reduce the pile by one will be seized upon.

Many forms are filled in on screen and then posted electronically to the employer. If you are adept at using computers and can access the form electronically, you may decide to complete it on screen. It can take a lot of time to space it correctly and arrange it properly, so do not feel you have to do this if it would not be easy for you. Be aware too that some employers like to see your handwriting, so will not mind at all if you complete this part of the form by hand.

Now let us take each of these sections in turn to see what kind of answer the employer is looking for from each one. The following sections usually appear on every application form.

## Personal details

The first section of the form is concerned with your personal details. These questions ask your name, address and other facts. You will not have any opportunity to 'sell yourself' here. You will normally be asked to give your first and second names in full and your address. You must give your home, work (if applicable) and mobile phone numbers. Always include a personal e-mail address if you have one, but think carefully before giving a work e-mail address unless you are confident that it is private enough or that your current employer will not object to this personal use.

You may have to state your nationality and sometimes answer further questions about your eligibility to work in this country. These questions are not being asked just out of curiosity. The employer needs to check that you are allowed to work here if offered the job. You may be asked for a description of your general state of health. An application for a Civil Service position may ask many more detailed questions about your background, including details about your parents and their backgrounds, whether you have ever had any other nationality, your place of birth and so on.

You may be asked where you saw the advertisement for the post. This is to tell the employer how effective the company's recruitment advertising is. It is helpful if you can give precise details.

Some people are tempted to include a recent head and shoulders photograph with their form. Unless this is specifically requested because physical appearance is relevant to the job, you should not do it. If your application is the only one with a photograph attached it will look very odd.

## Academic qualifications

You need to give the names and addresses of places where you have studied. The employer may want to know particulars of qualifications obtained (classes, divisions, etc) and the names of courses or subjects studied, if appropriate. If you have recently left school or college you will be expected to make more of this experience by giving full information about subjects taken or projects worked on.

Do not send in copies or originals of your exam certificates unless you are specifically asked to. A list of your qualifications will suffice at this stage. You may be asked to produce original documents once offered the job.

## Work experience

This section of the form is where you expand on your previous work experience. The aim is not just to produce a list of all the jobs that you have ever had, but rather to explain what skills and abilities you have to offer a new employer. Most space on the form will normally be allocated to your current or last job. This is on the understanding that the most recent job will probably be the one which afforded you most responsibility. You will often be asked for a brief outline of the duties performed, and sometimes the salary or wage that you were paid. You do not need to send in copies of payslips with your form, though. If you are employed at present you may be asked for details of the notice that you are required to give.

Most forms ask that previous jobs should be put in a logical order (usually, the most recent first) and you will be asked to give details of the posts held, the names and addresses of the employers, and the dates concerned. Sometimes you will be asked why you left each job and the salary at that time. In this case it is important that you give only *positive* reasons for leaving previous jobs. If you complain about former companies, colleagues or employers it will look as if you are a difficult person who is capable of running down this recruiting company in the future.

If you are really keen to leave or parted on bad terms from your last employer it can feel difficult to come up with anything upbeat about leaving, but it is an important part of presenting a constructive image of yourself. Here are some examples of positive reasons given for leaving a job:

■ 'I left to take up a new position.'

■ 'I embarked on a period of travel abroad.'

■ 'For family reasons, I moved to a different part of the country.'

■ 'I left work and went to college to resume my studies.'

■ 'I was offered a job with increased responsibility.'

## Interests

There may be a section where you are asked to outline your leisure interests and activities. You will need to show that you are a well-rounded person with a variety of hobbies or interests outside work. It helps to have some sporting or active interests and others which use your mind or involve creativity. A selection of different types of activities will show this and as many as eight pastimes could be mentioned. It does not matter if you have not done all the things on your list recently, as long as you would be happy to discuss them in an interview. This means that you must know about or be interested in every item that you write down here. Try to avoid a simple list of the interests in your life. You need to bring the things you spend time on alive, so that the reader can almost see you doing them.

Look at the following list on David's application form:

'Rugby, cricket, tennis, cinema, music, reading, gardening, gym.'

Now see how it becomes much more interesting once some examples and illustrations have been added to show how the interests feature in his life:

'I have designed my own garden and enjoy the ongoing challenges and opportunities that this interest provides. I go to the cinema regularly and particularly like foreign films. I listen to a wide variety of music in my spare time and spend time reading – including modern novels and classic literature. I like watching rugby, cricket and tennis and am a regular gym user. I have studied creative writing and gained a diploma in Short Story Writing.'

Consider what you are writing from the point of view of the person reading it, rather than resenting the time it takes to write material that you are already familiar with. This can be difficult if you have to fill in lots of application forms, but it can make a real difference to your chances of success, as it will help you to stand out from all the other applicants.

## Referees

You may be asked for particulars of two (or sometimes three) people to whom approaches may be made about your suitability for the work concerned and your character. These references are not normally taken up unless you are picked for the job, but you must always ask permission before you put anyone's name down as a referee. You will need a name, job title, e-mail address, full mailing address and telephone number for each person. In some cases, having a satisfactory reference is a prerequisite for the interview.

Do not put 'available at interview' or 'available on request' if asked for referees, as it will appear that you have something to hide. You must arrange for suitable referees to be available when you are completing any application form. One referee would usually be from your present or most recent workplace, normally the manager, supervisor or team leader to whom you reported or someone more senior. Some larger companies ask for all references to be provided by the human resources department. The referee should be able to talk about your performance in the workplace, give details of your health and absence record and give advice about the suitability of employing you in a particular role.

One referee can be a personal friend who can talk about your character. This should not be a member of your own family, and should preferably be someone with a reputable job of their own. Some referees of this type can be family friends, teachers or lecturers from college, church or community group contacts, or sometimes a doctor who knows you will agree to be your referee.

There are circumstances when it can be difficult to get people to provide references for you. If you left your last job because of personal difficulties there, it may be awkward to ask someone to be a referee for you. You could either ask someone from your previous place of work or put down two personal referees, that is, people known to you who can provide character references. Be aware though that a future employer may ask to contact your last place of work to ask about you.

Referees normally respond with a reference only when approached by a possible new employer. They will be sent a letter or a form to complete – sometimes before you have been invited to interview but normally afterwards.

The rest of any application form contains the questions that require more attention, with challenging subjects that need effort, creativity and attention to detail for their completion.

## Equal opportunities

You will sometimes find a question about equal opportunities for jobs with large corporations, major service providers, eg the police force or ambulance service, voluntary organizations, local authorities or charities. Any organization which works with the general public may be interested in your attitude to the issues raised by this subject. This kind of question is more difficult to answer. If you find a question such as 'What does equal opportunities mean to you?' on a form, it requires some thought. Like most difficult questions, there is no precise, correct answer, but the employer will want to know that you take the subject seriously. You need to illustrate this in your response by defining the phrase and saying how it is important to the job. One of the best ways is by using other words to explain it. You could say: 'Equal opportunities mean everyone getting the same chances in employment and access to services.'

In some cases the employer will go further and ask: 'How would you put equal opportunities into practice in this job?' Your answer should refer to the way that the services in question need to be accessible to all the people being served and what measures could be taken for ensuring that this happens. To give an impressive answer you will need to draw on your previous experience of this kind of work. What measures did you take in former workplaces to ensure that services were opened up to all clients? Have you observed particular examples of marketing, literature or service delivery that you think make a difference?

If you have not had direct experience of this kind of work before, then you need to think this question through in some detail. Why is the employer so interested in your views on this issue? What difference would an awareness of equal opportunities make to the client group that you would be dealing with? Treating people fairly applies to staff as well as clients, though, and you should also mention that you are keen to play your part as a sympathetic and supportive team member within the organization itself. If you can mention an example of the way you have worked with clients or colleagues that you feel illustrates your fair treatment of other people, this will count in your favour. Even if you do not have personal examples to quote you could mention examples of good practice you have seen or heard about.

## Statement by candidate

This section can appear in various guises. A typical form of words is: 'Give any other information which you consider will be helpful in support of your application.' Some versions split this question into several smaller questions such as 'What experience do you have that makes you suitable?', 'Describe the education and training you have received and why it is relevant to this post' and so on. This will normally be the biggest blank space on the form; it is the section generally left to last and it will require the most work.

Do not see completing this answer as a problem to be dreaded. Instead, view it as a gift – a way of summing up why you deserve to be called for an interview and a chance to really impress the employer. It is often better to type the answer to this question on a computer if you have access to one, as it normally represents a large block of words. You may find that the form provides a limited amount of space and invites you to 'Use additional sheets if necessary'. This generally means that you are expected to take up more space than has been provided on the form, and the employer assumes that to do the question justice you will need more paper. Use the space on the form to write 'Please see attached sheet(s),' and start your answer on extra paper that you can fix firmly to the finished form. Always include your name and contact details on each and every additional sheet that you use in case they get separated from your application form. If you are applying online, make the most of the space available. Unless a word limit is specified, in which case you must abide by it, the employer will be looking for a full answer here.

The most important point to remember is that the answer that you give should tell the employer what you think you can contribute to the organization, not why you want to work there. So you must find ways of stressing what you have to offer. Each candidate will be anxious to get the job because of the benefits that come with it, such as the wages, job security etc. What the employer wants to hear is how you can add to the work being done by the organization. Chapter 6 provides guidelines and examples of how to answer such questions.

You need to present your strong points which match the job requirements. Start by studying any information you have been sent by the employer. The most common documents sent out to accompany an application form are the job description and a person specification. These will have been written for the specific job you are applying for, so that applicants can be clear what is required and how they can best fulfil the requirements. If these documents are provided you must show you meet the criteria as written down, or you will automatically be rejected. If you have applied online, this stage can even be automated, with a computer analysing every form to check it meets the basic requirements before passing it to the next stage. Most employers start the filtering process by ticking off the elements of the job description and person specification that the applicant demonstrates. Often this level of screening applicants is performed by the personnel office or human resources department. The person doing this may not have any specialist knowledge of the job role concerned, so will only be able to take into account how far you show you match the written job requirements.

Here is a real example of such a question, together with the advice on the application form, and details of how to answer it:

'Relevant Experience, Skills and Abilities
You need to read the person specification for the job you are applying for carefully. For each point you will need to explain how your skills, abilities and experience make you suitable for this job. These may have been gained through previous jobs, voluntary or community work, spare-time activities and training. You should give examples of how

and where you have demonstrated these skills. It is not sufficient to say I can, I am able or I believe, etc. **What you write in this section will be used to decide whether or not to interview you for this job.** It will help the shortlisting panel if you can number your response to each of the points on the person specification form.'

Not only is this form stating clearly that the interview shortlist will be decided on whether candidates have shown they fit the person specification or not, it is asking that each point of your answer is given a number that corresponds to the same point on the person specification. The assessor will then literally tick a box when he or she has seen that you have satisfied each and every point that is specified as essential to do the job.

The instructions may be more mildly worded, as in this example:

'Please explain why you are applying for this vacancy and how you feel your transferable skills, relevant experience and achievements match the requirements for this role. Please make particular reference to the job description and person specification for the role.'

This is still clearly asking you to match up your background with the requirements of the job, and the candidates who get shortlisted for interview will have made sure that they answer each and every point in the job description and person specification before they submit their form. It can feel mechanical and uninspiring to plod through writing an application in this formulaic way, but you cannot expect a recruiter to do the matching-up work for you by searching through what you have written to see whether the specified criteria have been satisfied. You need to make it totally obvious that you are clearly capable of doing the job well by using the same terms and phrases as the employer.

If essential and desirable requirements are both listed, you may think that as long as you match up your experience with the essential requirements you will be invited for interview.

In fact this might not always be the case. In the event of a tie the desirable requirements will be taken into account to decide between two candidates, so the more of that list too that you can show matches your experience, the better your chances of being invited to the next stage of the process.

It may sound a boring activity but you need to deliberately work your way through each item listed and draft a short paragraph to say 'I am (whatever they have asked for), as demonstrated by (your relevant example)' to ensure you do not miss any of the points out. Do not assume that the employer will understand what you mean unless you explain fully. Saying you have five years' computing experience may not get you a tick against a job description which requires you to be fluent at using spreadsheets and database applications. You need to state specifically and clearly 'I have used the Excel spreadsheet package in my work for the last three years and am confident at entering and managing data to track orders and oversee customer activity.'

Your answer must:

■ demonstrate that you match each part of the person specification;

■ give examples to show that you have experience of every component of the job description;

■ highlight skills and experience that may not be directly asked for, but that you feel are relevant, explaining why you think so;

■ describe your personality and why you think you would be good in the job and what you would add to the team.

From studying the advertisement and information provided about the job, you should be able to highlight these requirements and ensure that, as far as possible, you satisfy them. Remember that you can describe your work experience in different ways, depending on the exact nature of the position concerned. For example, in one case you may emphasise the experience you obtained in handling people and achieving results. In another case, you may need to emphasise the amount of work you did, analysing and interpreting data, preparing reports and contributing to the development of new ideas, policies and procedures. Detail about the precise way in which you worked is not required. What are relevant to the employer are the transferable skills involved in each case, ie those skills that will be equally useful in the job you are applying for now.

Employers are interested in three main areas:

■ your skills;

■ your experience;

■ your personality.

You may be asked about your career ambitions. You should convey enthusiasm about the job and imply that you will want to progress within the company without seeming to have way-out or aggressive ambitions.

Here are some more examples of questions that you could find on an application form:

■ Can you describe a time when you have influenced other people?

■ Give examples of when you have worked effectively with others.

■ Tell us three things that have shaped the person you are today.

■ What have been the major successes in your work to date?

■ What relevant skills are you bringing to this post?

■ Why do you think you are suited to this position?

■ What specific factors attract you to this job?

## Mind the gap!

We all have aspects of our history which need some explaining. It may involve a time when you were not working for some reason, or a job which ended more abruptly than you would have liked. Whether it is a period of unemployment, some time in prison or detention, or being sacked from a position, you will need to explain, in the most positive way, what happened to you during that time.

This can present a challenge if we are talking about being laid off, a period of unemployment or time spent in detention, but it is vital that you have a story to tell about your experience. As you draft your response to a question about this period, think about what positive aspects came out of it. Concentrate on what you learnt, how you spent time productively and be able to describe any steps you have taken to move on in your life.

It may be that you have not spent time thinking about this at all so far. Imagine the anxieties that an employer could have about someone who has been sacked, is unemployed or has been out of the labour market for some time. They may see you as unskilled, unemployable or rusty and difficult to work with. Collate any information and evidence you can to counter these worries. Show that you get on well with people as a rule, have kept your skills up to date and would be an asset to any team.

## Monitoring form

Some employers will send you another form to complete with your application form. It asks for details of your ethnic origin and if you have any disabilities. Often the form will explain what it will be used for: 'The information contained in this form will help us to monitor the percentage of applicants that we employ from different ethnic groups. On receipt of your application it is filed separately and will not be considered in conjunction with your application'. Sometimes applicants worry that this information may prejudice the employer against them, but this is not the case. The employer is just trying to find out how fair their recruitment policies are and the information will help them to put their equal opportunities policy into practice.

## Acknowledgement card

You may find a card has been enclosed with your application form. This is for you to complete with your name and address so that the employer can send it back to you when he or she receives your application. Normally, only large companies are this well organized, so put a stamp on it and return it to them with your application. You will know that your form has arrived safely when the card is posted back to you.

## Points to remember

1.  Establishing a clear idea of the kind of organization the vacancy is with will enable you to think more easily about the job and how you would fit in. Study any information about the company, especially its website and publicity materials.

2.  Always start by working to any information provided about the job, especially the job description and person specification. Unless you can prove that you meet all the points they contain, you will not be invited for interview.

3.  Pay just as much attention to the 'easy' bits of the form as to the more 'difficult' parts. Errors or omissions anywhere may limit your chances of success.

## Dos and don'ts

✔ Do write the form out in rough first.

✔ Do use a computer to type your written statement.

✔ Do give examples where possible as evidence of your claims.

✘ Don't attempt to type the whole form unless you are a confident, skilled and accurate typist.

✘ Don't tell lies on your form – you can be sacked if you are subsequently found out.

✘ Don't leave the more difficult questions so late that you do not have time to complete them impressively.

# Presentation

The way in which you complete your form is regarded by employers as very important. The vital lesson regarding presentation to learn from this book is: *the way that your form looks is as crucial as what you have written on it, particularly if submitted in hard copy*. When your application lands on an employer's desk or in his or her inbox, he or she will give it a three-second glance to gain a first impression before deciding whether it is worth studying more closely. The most comprehensive and well thought-out forms can be ruined because of lack of time and trouble taken to fill them in. No matter how good a candidate you are in theory, if your form does not look neat and easy to read, you are unlikely to be considered for the job.

I have seen many untidy and messy forms which have been carelessly completed with too little time dedicated to the task. Some employers would simply discard such a form without even reading it.

You may think that companies would be so interested in the content of a form that the way it looked was less important than what it contained. Unfortunately, bad presentation, however nice the writing, makes it a trial to read, particularly when there is a pile of 50 other forms waiting in line to be looked at.

Be aware that particular jobs mean that employers may look

for different signs of your potential from your application. With any job concerned with administration, writing or paper-work of any kind the employer will be ruthless about the way that your answers are written. When I recruited people to work with job-seekers, I expected all the applicants to submit beauti-fully prepared CVs to show they had expertise in this area to offer to other people. Similarly, employers offering work concerned with art and design matters will notice the details of your presentation. You should pay particular attention to the way that you space and lay out your writing for this type of work to let the employer know that you have ability and skills in visual presentation.

Employers considering applicants for figure work, accounting or finance jobs will be looking for correct details and clear, careful, neat writing. You may be using the computer or calculators much of the time in the job, but the characteris-tics of care and clarity will still be extremely important. The way you complete the form will give an insight into the way you are likely to perform in the job.

The key to a well-presented document is planning and prepa-ration. Although it takes time, if submitting a form in hard copy you should never fill it in straight away without composing a rough draft first. This means that you can make your mistakes on the rough version and only when you are happy with your answers copy them on to your neat, final version, when there will be much less likelihood of errors creeping in. Use lined paper under the final version so that you can keep the lines straight and always use a ruler to underline, end a section or delete information. If you do make an error, cross it through neatly with a single line or use correction fluid to make an invisible repair. Little details like this can mean the difference between success and failure.

## Spelling

Bad spelling is inexcusable on application forms and will normally mean that your application will not be read right through, even if it is for a job that does not require a great deal of written expertise. This may seem unfair but if you know that your spelling and grammatical skills are weak, make sure that you check all the difficult words by using a dictionary and allow extra time to get a good speller to check the form through thoroughly for you.

If you are applying for a job which involves writing and know you are weak in this area, you may want to get some help to improve your spelling and grammar, for example at an evening class. It is never too late to learn and you will find local colleges are full of people just like you who are improving their confidence and their job chances by continuing with their education in this way.

Employers and recruiters have told me that if they are confronted with a form that contains errors and spelling mistakes, they will often not even bother to read it through. The applicant may be perfect for the job in every other respect but it will all be to no avail. Bad presentation puts people off in a big way. Given a bad-looking form, the employer will make automatic judgements about you, such as:

■ You do not give adequate time to your preparation.

■ You are not prepared to check the details of your work.

■ You do not know the importance of good communication.

■ You may not be willing to learn and develop new skills.

■ You could end up being an embarrassment to the organization.

None of these things may be true, but they are significant enough impressions to mean that your application goes straight into the reject pile. Don't let this be your fate. Improve your spelling and your literacy levels and you will increase your job chances.

Most employers now have an electronic version of every application form available via their website. You can read the whole application pack on-line and download (receive and store on your computer) any part or all of it. This means that there are three ways of applying. You can fill the form in on screen, press 'Send' and submit it that way; you can access it locally, work at it and reshape it on your own computer and then e-mail it back; or finally, you can print out the form, work on it at home and then post it off. Whichever way you choose, if you are sending it in by computer you must be extremely careful not to make the two classic mistakes. The first is to send it in only partly completed. This is extremely easy to do. You are working through the form, you get to a tricky part and you think 'I'll just come back to that and finish it off later.' Because you cannot see the whole form on the screen at once, it is just too simple to forget to ever fill in that missing information, leaving the employer to try and guess what this means. The second mistake is to send the form in as soon as you finish it, leaving it unchecked for any errors.

## Using computers

Computers and scanners have transformed the way application forms can be completed for those who have access to such equipment and who are confident and skilled at using it. If you scan a form, make sure you keep to the original amount of space provided as far as possible, tempting though it is to stretch the form out to fit your needs. Remember that the reason the employer is using an application form is to be able to compare candidates easily, so if your form ends up looking markedly different from all the others, yours may not be considered.

If you are using a computer without a scanner, copy out the form exactly as it is on the paper and try to use the most similar typeface or font that you can find, so that it does not look as though you have altered the form. Once you have all the headings in place you can type in your answers and print out the form. Many people use a combination of handwriting and typing to complete their forms. They will fill in by hand all the factual questions about their personal details and employment experience and use a computer to type out the rest. This means that the longer questions such as 'Why are you applying for this post?' will have 'Please see attached sheet' on the form, together with the completed answer typed out on a plain piece of paper inserted into the final document with a paper clip or a staple. If you include extra pages in this way make sure that they are very clearly labelled as belonging to you and mark each sheet with the job details, for example job title and reference number if there is one, in case they get separated from the main form.

Increasingly employers put their application forms on their organization's website so that they can be downloaded direct from the internet. This means you can access forms immediately without having to request them and then wait for them to be posted to you. They can often be sent back to the company electronically too, just by you completing them on screen and redirecting them back.

## Improving your writing

If you have to fill in a hard copy form and you know your handwriting is untidy, you must allow extra time for this part of the process. Would your writing be improved by using capital (or upper-case) letters all the way through the form? It is difficult to write in straight lines in an empty box. Put lined paper underneath the form so that the lines show through and act as a guide. Alternatively, you can pencil fine lines on the form itself, as long as you remember to rub them out carefully before you send off the finished application. A black pen should always be used as blue ink does not show up well if the form is photocopied (for other people in the company). Make sure that the pen you use does not blotch and smudge on the paper by using a good quality ink pen.

## Style

Writing neatly on the form is important, but so are ordering the contents logically and making the key points stand out. It is difficult enough to absorb any information from the printed page and trying to conjure up a picture of an individual from answers on a form is even more problematic. Yet that is what employers are trying to do when they read your form. Therefore it makes sense to think through in some detail what you want to convey. The best answers are not written straight on to the page but considered and arranged carefully, well before the act of writing them down.

Some applicants think that they should change their style of writing to make it more formal and they try to include long and complicated words that they would not normally use. Far from impressing the reader, this can sound stilted and old-fashioned, which is probably not the way that you want it to appear. You can be confident that if you write as though you are talking directly to the reader, you will sound fine. The important thing to concentrate on, as far as style is concerned, is that your writing is easy to read and understand.

You cannot assume that the reader knows what you are talking about unless you have explained it clearly and simply. You should aim to tread the fine line between giving enough detail and ensuring that you are concise in your explanations. The main constraint is normally the space allowed for your answers. The use of note form or bullet points can help with this.

## Layout

Think about the layout of the writing on the page when you are filling in your first rough copy. Each piece of information should be enclosed in its own border of white space to keep it visually separate from the next item. The contents of your form can be made to look more attractive and eye-catching with the judicious use of underlining, so make your qualifications and job titles stand out from the rest of the information presented. Bullet points can also be used to show the key elements.

## Additional sheets of paper

If the application form invites you to 'continue on a separate sheet of paper if necessary', it is best to do so. The employer is indicating that he or she thinks it likely that you will need more space than that provided to give an adequate answer. Most of the other applicants will be using the extra space allowed, so your answer will look brief in comparison if you do not do the same.

It makes sense to keep a supply of stationery if you are applying for jobs. Good quality envelopes and paper make a difference to the way your application looks and mean that you are never without the 'tools' to apply for a job that comes up. However, do ensure that you always use the same colour paper as the original form (usually white) if you are sending in extra pages of your own.

Do not use any coloured paper that is darker than ivory or cream, as it will not photocopy clearly and your answers may be obscured if copies need to be made once the application has been received.

## Some common problems

### 'My writing is too big to fit into the space provided.'

You can reduce the size of your script for this purpose. The advantage in completing your form on a rough copy first is that you can spend time arranging your answers to fit the form. You must scale down your writing to ensure that you have room to answer adequately, even if you need several attempts to get it small enough. It is preferable to use smaller writing than your normal style, to ensure that you put enough detail in your answers.

Compare the size of your writing with that of other people's. If yours is bigger, you may well be offering an employer less information than other applicants in your answers. You should also look at exactly what information you are including. Can you alter what you have drafted to make it more concise and snappy? Perhaps you could use bullet points and summaries rather than full sentences. Draft and redraft what you are putting down so that you end up with leaner prose to say what you mean more effectively.

## 'My experience doesn't seem to tally with what the job requires.'

It may be that the job is not suitable for you, in which case you need to do more thinking about the sort of work you are looking for. It is difficult to get a job when you really have no relevant qualifications, experience or attributes. If you are trying to break into a new career you will need to prove that, although different, your previous experience has given you the type of skills that will be transferable enough to enable you to make a contribution to the company concerned.

For instance, if you have managed projects before but the position is looking for someone who has had experience of managing staff, you will need to be able to show that the skills that you have developed are similar to the ones they are looking for. You surely have to plan the projects you are responsible for now, and timetable a schedule of work; communicating the key aims and point of your projects may be a priority; if a team works with you, you may have to liaise between all the different parties; and thorough project management will involve monitoring progress, evaluation and review. You may have had to motivate people at various times during the project and offer feedback on the performance of others. This list represents skills that are essential to managing a team of people, even if you cannot claim to have run your own team so far.

## 'I have only just left college and don't have any real work experience yet.'

The challenge here is to minimize your weakness – that you have not yet worked – and maximize your experiences at college. It need not be just formal work experience that counts in this situation. You could offer experience of voluntary work or part-time jobs as substitutes. Helping out in a local project can show that you have commitment to a certain type of work and that you have picked up the skills demanded in the job you are applying for. Use this time when you are making applications to start some kind of part-time or voluntary work so that you will not have the same problem in the future.

It is extremely rare for employers to take someone on with no work experience at all. Recognize the fact that you need to build up a bank of working skills to provide evidence that you will be valuable in a paid job. Even if all your experience is in a voluntary role, this could make the difference between you and another candidate. You can benefit in the long term by volunteering with an organization with aims you share. You may never have worked in a voluntary capacity before but the experience of offering your voluntary labour can enhance your career in all sorts of ways. You may get access to training opportunities and the chance to gain new and transferable skills. You will become more positive when you have a useful contribution to make and ambitious for your future if you use your time wisely in this way. Voluntary work could also provide you with good references and contacts, and confidence in your own abilities.

Work experience placements undertaken at school or college can also be used to show how you were able to apply yourself in a work role.

## 'I didn't do well at school and don't have any qualifications to put down.'

You need not worry about this as long as you have something

else to offer the employer. Any work experience that you have can show that you learn quickly, apply yourself and can fit in working in a disciplined environment. If you feel you could now benefit from a second chance at education, then enrolling on a local college course will always look impressive to future employers. Not everyone is best suited to taking exams at 16, and you may find that returning to learning at a later stage enables you to have a much more successful experience with studying.

## 'I just can't get excited about the job. I keep putting off the task of filling in the form.'

This is a very common experience with application forms. It may be necessary to consider whether this job is really the one for you. If you have spent some time thinking about the form and how your skills, personality and experience are suitable for it, and yet still cannot work up any enthusiasm for the task, perhaps it is not worth bothering. Many application forms are thrown away without being completed because the applicants find the closing date has arrived and they have made little or no progress with the form.

On the other hand, we all find filling in application forms hard and lonely work, and this often makes the task seem daunting. Most people underestimate the time needed to do the job properly and simply run out of time. It may be that you need to devote more creativity and energy to the task. You really have to summon up all your confidence and pride in order to sell yourself to the employer and be ready to take at least as many days as there are pages in the form to do it justice. Shut yourself away from all distractions, turn the television off, concentrate solely on the form and tell yourself how good you'll feel when it is done and returned to the employer. Don't let the chance of a good job pass you by for the lack of some hard work.

Just making a start is always the hardest and most challenging part, especially if you do not normally have to do a lot of written work and you have not filled in a form for a long time. Don't let the look of all those blank pages overwhelm you. We all have to go through the same thing to get the job we want. Spending enough time thinking through the job and how you can fit into the role can help you get more enthused about the prospect.

When you are ready to start writing, using a copy of an old form you completed in the past may help save time and trouble for the factual parts of the form, which ask for information about education and previous places of work. Have your CV to hand at all times, if you have one, as this can provide a great deal of the information that you will need. Just complete a little bit to get you going and then have a break. Come back determined to tackle the next small section of the form. You will soon find that you are making progress and the task will not seem so impossible.

## 'Some of my answers only fill in a few lines when the space provided on the form is huge.'

This probably means that you have not spent enough time preparing your answers. The space given usually corresponds to the size of the answer that you are expected to give. All the other candidates will be making sure that they use all the available space, and your form needs to match. Imagine your form being considered along with the others. If yours obviously has shorter answers, it may be rejected without being read. You will need to start planning your answers again, this time going into much more detail about what you have achieved, what you know and what you can contribute. Think through all the aspects of the job, paying particular attention to all the information provided by the employer. Pick the brains of friends and relatives about what other relevant information you could include. Try researching similar jobs on the internet for more ideas about what could be important: www.connexions-direct.com/jobs4u can provide you with a wealth of information about many different types of work. Use the site to look up the kind of job you are applying for to give you more ideas about what to include. Do not worry about putting too much in, just concentrate on expanding your answers to increase the quantity of information.

## 'Even making my writing as small as possible, I need more space than that provided on the form.'

It may be that you started filling in the form without doing a rough copy first in order to work out the spacing required. If the form you are completing is really inadequate for the answers you think are required, you may have to use a separate sheet of paper but do make sure that you are not being long-winded in your answers. You should try to make your replies as concise and simple as possible otherwise you may lose your reader's attention. It will not look impressive if yours is the only application that keeps needing more space for every question. Try using bullet points instead of full sentences and be rigorous about just highlighting the key points in each answer.

## 'I have filled in all my personal details on the form but cannot complete the question about my personality strengths. It's too hard.'

This is one of the most important questions on the form. Employers may well appoint a candidate who does not have all the desired experience on the basis of his or her personality. You need to spend more time thinking about yourself and the sort of person the organization is looking for. Use the exercise on page 42 to give you some help and rack your brain to collect all the ideas you can about the sort of person you are. Ask friends and relatives for suggestions – but remind them that you only want to hear *good* comments about you at your best!

In reality, the whole point of the application process is to find out your answer to this question. Skills can be developed on the job and experience can be gained over time, training can increase competence and new ways of working can be learnt. Most of us don't change our personality to fit a job though. Our attitudes, outlook, energy and motivation tend to be fixed. People can be gregarious extroverts, reflective team members, active self-starters or studious theorists, and each different type will fit in better than another in a particular workplace.

The hardest part is coming up with a picture of what you are like. How would past colleagues and bosses describe you? At the times from the past when you really felt you were performing well and using all your strengths, what were you like then? List some words that describe you at your best in work, or look back at the list on page 43 of this book and form these words into sentences that sum you up. Try to concentrate on the type of person who would be wanted for the job you are applying for and mould your words to show that you would match this. You need to plug away at this as it could get you the job you want. Once you have composed a couple of paragraphs, you will be able to use this information when applying for future jobs too.

## 'I have finished the rough copy of my form but I am nervous that it may still have mistakes in it, even after I've checked it through.'

It is possible to spend so long poring over the document that it becomes impossible to see how well you have done. Have a rest from it for a while and do something totally different. Then come back to the task. Imagine that you have never seen the document before. Does it look well laid out and inviting to a reader? Is your writing tidy and neatly displayed? Are the main points of the form highlighted clearly but unfussily? Show the draft to friends and ask them to check it, and invite their comments on the way you have completed the answers and the way the form looks as a whole. If they agree it looks fine then settle for that, complete the final version and send it off, secure in the knowledge that you have done your best. Always take a copy of the finished version, or at least keep your rough draft, so you can remember exactly what you put on the form if you are invited to attend an interview and to save you time completing similar forms in the future.

Once you have sent off the form, try to forget about it until the date by which you will hear if you have been shortlisted.

## 'I have filled in several applications recently. To save time and effort, can I just copy out one of my previous ones to do most of the work when completing the one I received today?'

The answer is yes – and no. Yes, you can use earlier forms to complete the factual parts of the form, which normally cover your personal details, your education and your employment. However, be very careful to read the latest form properly before you rush ahead with this, as the way the questions are worded may be quite different. You will look careless if you give the places you worked in date order when the current form wants the latest job given first followed by the others in reverse order. So check everything before you copy or cut and paste it onto the new form.

No, do not use the old form for the other, more complex questions about why you want the job, what you have to offer and why you think you would be the most suitable candidate. The jobs are likely to be different each time even if the roles are similar, and the company or organization is always going to be different for each job you apply for. Even if you are making a second application for the same job in the same company, you would need to make some alterations as it will be necessary to improve your form if it was not successful the first time you applied. Thinking through the position afresh for each application means that your words will seem more appropriate and immediate to the reader when the application arrives.

## Points to remember

1. You only get one chance to make a good first impression, so if you are serious about wanting the job, commit yourself to putting in the best application you can.

2. Time spent making the form look presentable may give you an advantage when the shortlist for interview is being considered.

3. Work out exactly what you want to include before creating your final version.

## Dos and don'ts

✔ Do write in capital letters if your form is handwritten.

✔ Do spread information out on the page to make it easier to read.

✔ Do always check your spelling – errors could put the employer off entirely.

✘ Don't change your normal self-expression – try to write as you would talk.

✘ Don't worry if your answers don't come easily straight away – writing original material is a creative task that can sometimes be difficult at first.

✘ Don't give up if you face obstacles – this may be the right job for you, so keep trying to complete the form before the deadline.

# 6

# Guidelines and examples

The following examples show different questions frequently asked on application forms and explain how you should approach your answers.

## Please describe your main non-work or non-academic interests and tell us why these give you particular satisfaction.

This question is asking about your hobbies and interests but it will not be enough just to give a list. You will need to say why you pursue these interests and what you do with your time. Ideally, your answer should indicate how these interests add to the contribution you could make to the organization. For instance:

'I am a member of the Northern Cycling Club and regularly participate in group rides. I believe that non-motorized transport is beneficial for the environment and I act as publicity officer for the Club to encourage more cycleways in cities and to attract more members.'

'I have played and watched football for the last twenty years. I attend my local team's matches whenever possible and coach local youngsters in the season. It is satisfying to help foster talent in other people in this way.'

'I am skilled at baking cakes and make elaborate ones for friends and family when there is a special occasion. I won a prize for an Easter cake last year and was featured in the local paper as a result.'

'I read modern novels as a way of relaxing after work. I have recently started a reading group with seven friends and neighbours to discuss and analyse selected books together.'

## What has been your greatest achievement to date?

You must choose what to answer for yourself here, but think why the employer is asking this question. He or she will make a judgement not so much about the example you give, but about why you think of it as an achievement.

Some ways of answering could include:

'Bringing up my family has to be my greatest achievement. I am proud of the fact that I have good relationships with all three children now they are older and I always make it my first priority to keep a good atmosphere between everybody.'

This tells the employer that the candidate is likely to be a helpful person to have around the office – someone who is sensitive to others and who can perhaps stop team conflict before it arises.

'At school I studied a vocational course in the sixth form. Part of the course involved a study of a local factory and I found that I learnt a lot. At the end of the work I had to give a presentation to my whole year group. I rehearsed in front of a couple of friends first and they gave me helpful feedback and encouragement. Despite feeling sick with nerves before I went on, I did my best and now will not feel so shy if I have to talk to a big group again. I learnt that doing plenty of preparation helps you to feel more confident about managing the task.'

This indicates a completely different approach from a younger applicant, and shows that the candidate demonstrated courage, was determined and quick to learn from the experience.

'I went trekking in the Himalayas during my gap year. It was a terrifying prospect and yet turned out to be an exhilarating experience. I did not think I could cope with the journey at one stage, but the thing that pulled me through was the terrific team work from the group who went. We looked after each other, helped each other to exceed our initial expectations, and are all still firm friends nearly five years later.'

This applicant has an unusual achievement to describe, but its significance is the strength of a good team in problem solving and supporting its members. This understanding will be of use in any workplace, and indicates the writer will be keen to play a full part in any group activities.

'I have been a voluntary trustee of a local charity for the last three years, after the Chair asked me to join to help with fundraising. It has been a varied experience with several difficult periods when our funding nearly ran out. I enjoy keeping the staff morale as positive as possible and using my skills to bring more money in for a good cause. I am proud to have kept up my involvement even though volunteering on top of a day job is never easy. I know I help to keep the organization going.'

This answer demonstrates several things. The candidate is someone who will maintain her effort even when the going gets tough, is motivated by helping others, and will be the person who will give extra effort for the stated aims of the organization. She sounds like a valuable person to have around at work.

'I was put in charge of a major office relocation at work. We needed to move premises to save money and it meant that two offices had to be combined into one new one. The arrangements needed to be agreed by everyone in order to make it all go smoothly and so that everyone was happy. The communications about the proposals and the progress of the move were by far the most time-consuming, difficult but important part of the project. We are all now in the new place and my manager gave me a special bonus recently in recognition of my extra contribution to ensuring the move went so well.'

This candidate sounds like a useful person to have in any team. She understands the importance of communicating well with others in order to make projects succeed, and can handle a difficult brief. She enjoys taking responsibility and has shown that she is appreciated by her present employer.

'I work in the IT team and am a member of the help-desk staff. Recently we introduced a new computer system across the organization and because of circumstances beyond our control, on the day the new system went live there were huge problems across the whole organization. The system kept failing and people were losing important work all over the place. The helpline phones were red-hot with complaints and cries for help. It was getting too difficult for us to respond properly so I took it upon myself to draft an urgent e-mail to everyone to explain what was happening and to reassure all staff that we were going to solve the problem soon. My manager was pleased with the memo and we sent it out. Later I was told that it had

helped a lot to reduce the levels of panic when people real-
ized it was a wider problem and not just their own work
station that had gone wrong.'

Someone who can rise above general mayhem sounds like a
good team member. Taking the initiative is often a good thing,
but so is checking with your boss before rushing ahead with
the idea. This candidate seems to be cool under pressure,
proactive about making changes and thoughtful on behalf of
other people. Most managers would be glad to have a person
like this in a large IT department.

'I moved house last year. This was a big event for me, as I
had to do it alone having recently divorced. I made the
decisions, carried out the arrangements and organized the
whole transition. One sale fell through at the last minute,
so I had to start all over again. Eventually I found somewhere suitable. It has meant a lot of changes which did not
feel easy at first but now I am happier and more settled
and am not scared of moving again if need be.'

This is a more individual example, which relates to a domestic
achievement. Moving house is something that most of us have
to deal with at some point. It ranks as a very high-stress event.
This applicant tells us she used courage and strength of character to carry out the move, and that she experienced personal
growth and development as a result. She is obviously someone
who keeps calm, handles stress well and is very purposeful.

'I left school last year and did well in my A levels. I was
not sure how it would all turn out as my mother died
when I was taking my mock exams, and although she had
been ill for a while, I found it difficult to carry on as usual
with my school work. My teachers were very helpful and
understanding and I slowly applied myself to my revision
again. I got the grades I was expected to and feel proud of
myself for managing that, despite all the upset and shock.'

This candidate certainly had to prove his resilience and determination in the light of his bereavement. He pulled out all the stops and his good grades are all the more praiseworthy as a result.

You can see from the examples above that it is not the specifics of the achievements that are the impressive aspect. It is the general attitude shown, the lessons learnt or the journey travelled that stand out. Spend time thinking about your life and background. What achievements would you quote for a question such as this? Be careful of using very personal examples unless you are sure that you would be happy to discuss them in more detail in an interview later on. It may be one thing to write about the death of a close relative and quite a different one to have to talk about it in front of strangers when you are trying to appear positive and upbeat.

## Please give your reasons for applying for this post.

Of all the questions on any application form, this is the one that will determine whether you should be called for an interview or not. It asks the question that the recruiters really want answered. It can also be deceptive. By asking for your reasons for applying for the post, it implies that your own motivation and career ambitions are of interest to the employer. They are not. What the employer actually wants to know is: what particular contribution would you make to this organization?

All applicants have their own reasons for applying for any job. These could include:

■ wanting an increase in salary;

■ applying for a promotion;

■ wanting a job in a different location;

■ being keen to work for a reputable company;

■ wanting to take on more responsibility;

■ having less travel time;

- getting out of the present job;

- accessing more training opportunities;

- moving to a different team of people;

- wanting to make a change in life.

But most recruiters are not particularly interested in knowing what you want from the job they are offering. They want to know what they will gain from employing you.

Jeff is a senior officer in a health trust. He tells us:

'It is a real turn-off when people go on about what they want from working here on their forms. I know that every application is completed by someone who wants the job or they would not have applied for it. So don't go on about what you stand to gain. I won't be giving you the job for the sake of your career advancement or satisfaction but because I think you will bring the most to the post. That means you have to spell out for me very clearly what you have to offer that the other applicants don't.'

So when you are faced with this question on the form do not underestimate the effort you need to put into responding to it. You need to put yourself in the place of the recruiter and shape your answer to impress them.

This question gives you every opportunity to craft a relevant, comprehensive and an inspiring picture of what you believe you can contribute to the job. The way that you answer this question depends on the sort of position applied for, but here are some examples:

'I am applying for this post because I am a skilled technician and believe that I have a lot to contribute to the job. In my present role I work closely with the pharmacist on duty and make sure that the supplies of drugs and medicines are clearly and safely displayed. I am a hard-working member of the team and can cope with an uneven pressure of work. I communicate well with my superiors and colleagues at all times. I enjoy this work very much and would relish the opportunity to contribute to the service provided by the General Hospital.'

This candidate makes a clear case for the contribution he can make, explaining the significance of his personality to doing the job very well.

'I have worked in the retail sector for the last five years and am keen to move into a managerial position. I have been on a first-level supervisors' course and found it very helpful. I stand in for my manager when he is away and have found the team respond to me very well. I always consult them before taking major decisions, and they know that I will be fair but firm in the way I manage. I enjoy motivating others to work better and find it easy to help sort out any misunderstandings between people.'

This applicant makes the most of her limited supervisory experience to show that she could deal with the major aspects of a management job, dealing with people, decision making and motivating her staff.

'The organization is moving into a very exciting period with the transition to the new structure. The power to inspect the private sector as well as the public will ensure that patients receive high-quality treatment wherever that treatment is located. I am particularly keen to come and join the team now as it has recently begun reviewing ambulance services. One of my responsibilities as a junior reporter was to maintain contact with my local ambulance station, and I feel I could bring some valuable insights to your reports into this area as a result.'

This applicant is making links between his recent work experience and the position to show how he has special skills that make his application stand out. He is demonstrating that he has something that the other candidates do not, to ensure that he is called for an interview.

## What do you think you would like/dislike most about this job?

When answering this type of question be careful that you do not labour on about the problems to be encountered. Employers want to know that potential candidates are keen and enthusiastic, so a long list of how enjoyable you would find the work will help here. It is fine to be aware of potential difficulties with a job as long as you present them as challenges to be overcome, preferably with suggestions for how to solve them rather than insurmountable obstacles.

Spend some time considering all aspects of the job, looking carefully at any information you have been sent about the post. This question gives you a chance to show that you are clear about the range of responsibility you will face. Just make sure you are positive about the opportunities that will be available should you get the job.

## Is there anything about your health record that you feel we should know?

This type of question is often asked when good health is a requirement of the job. You must use your common sense about the extent to which you reveal your medical history, but if any past illnesses are completely recovered from or would have no effect on your ability to do the job, they need not be mentioned. Be aware that if you do discuss some medical problem on the form, the employer will take it into account when considering your application, so the onus is on you to reassure him or her that you could do the job perfectly well, if this is the case.

## Any question relating to time not accounted for, including unemployment.

This type of question is looking for evidence that you have spent your time profitably. Even if you have been out of work for a long spell, you should be able to show that you have picked up new skills, or perhaps travelled or done some voluntary work while looking for a job.

'I was made redundant from my last job after a major reorganization process. I took the chance to get involved with a local volunteer scheme clearing out a disused play-space. We gained lottery money so that we could redesign and re-equip the area for local youngsters. The project finished last month and the play area is now in full use. It was launched by the local MP and the event was highlighted in the papers. I learnt a lot about how to get local initiatives up and running, and am now involved in a committee to reclaim more spaces in our area.'

Now let's look at the answers to two questions taken from a real application form. The job being applied for was an art teacher in a secondary school. The first question asks for information about the candidate's interests and hobbies and which of these the applicant might be able to offer as an after-school club. The second question asks why the candidate is applying for the job and why he or she should be considered for it.

# Application form – version A

## Other interests and activities

Please give information about any interests, hobbies or activities in which you are involved. Please indicate any activities that you would like to offer as an after-school club and indicate standard, where appropriate.

---

I am interested in Contemporary Art and I make a point of visiting galleries in central London regularly. I also have an interest in many areas of design, including contemporary architecture and sustainable design.

I enjoy keeping fit: I love to run, walk in the country, swim and ski when I get the opportunity. I regularly practise yoga and would consider offering it as a club.

I think green issues are important and I am involved with my community green group.

I like to read contemporary novels. I knit and sew for fun. I think a knitting club might be a possibility at the school.

_____

_____

_____

_____

_____

_____

_____

## Your interest in this post

Please state why you are applying for this post and say what particular attributes, qualities or special areas of interest or expertise you would bring to it. (Use the continuation sheet if necessary.)

I am a very well-qualified and experienced teacher who has a keen interest in silk screen printing. My background at the Thames College of Art and as an illustrator has enabled me to develop my own work using a silk screen mono print technique. I learned valuable technical skills from my first job in a printers when I left school. At College I was able to teach screen printed textiles very successfully to all GCSE groups.

I take great pride in being a very well-organized person who is a hard-working and conscientious team member. I enjoy using computers as a tool for administration and creative work.

I have a genuine enthusiasm for my subject and a talent for teaching. I love to use my skills and experience to motivate others and enjoy helping to open up the world of creative thinking to them. I am good humoured and patient, even under pressure.

I teach in a focused and firm manner, always trying to raise standards, but I am also a good listener with a calm understanding of some of the difficulties that students can face. Many ex-pupils have remained in contact with me over the years, saying that appreciation of the many facets of the art world has made a great impact on their lives.

This is a perfectly competent application and may possibly have taken the candidate on to the next stage of the recruitment process. However, we are in the middle of an economic downturn where there are many new people on the job market. Although teaching jobs are not under threat, there may well be more candidates applying for these more secure jobs.

I was not convinced that this candidate had made out the best case she could to get this job so I set her the challenge of filling up the boxes completely, making her statements more vivid and working on the tone of her answers to increase the image of her as a persuasive and dynamic applicant. For the first question, I asked her to go into more detail and what she likes about her interests and to talk more about how she would offer a club in the subject, why would pupils like to learn it, etc. I wanted enthusiasm and energy to come bouncing off the page.

For the second (vital) question, I asked her to write more about how she knows she is a good teacher, how she establishes a love of art in her pupils and why being well organized is important to her. In addition, I asked her specifically what ideas she had about how she would teach at this school, how art teaching is changing and what made her a better teacher than the next applicant.

Now look at version B of the application form, which gives the same answers after they had been revised and embellished.

## Application form – version B

### Other interests and activities

Please give information about any interests, hobbies or activities in which you are involved. Please indicate any activities that you would like to offer as an after-school club and indicate standard, where appropriate.

I have a deep interest in Contemporary Art which developed due to an inspiring teacher when I was at school. I make a point of visiting Tate Modern and The Whitechapel Gallery in central London regularly. I also have an interest in many areas of design, including contemporary architecture and sustainable design. Peter Huhn and Carl Winkworth are taking this latter area forward to new and exciting dimensions with their large-scale art projects based in nature.

I enjoy keeping fit: I love to run, walk in the country, swim and ski when I get the opportunity. I regularly practise yoga and would consider offering it as a co-curricular contribution. Pupils can see the benefits of yoga if it is combined with keep fit and some aerobic work on mats. I would like to initiate a school fitness challenge to embed healthy exercise as a lifestyle choice.

I think green issues are important and am an active member of my community green group. We are starting a community allotment programme in the local park, we organize family bulb-planting days and hold regular environmental awareness lectures, open to everyone. Getting people involved in doing something to enhance the common spaces is the key to increasing understanding of, and commitment to, these issues.

I like to read contemporary novels, my favourite authors are Ali Smith and John Bakeburn. I knit and sew for fun and am working on some of my own creations. I would be keen to set up a knitting club. Knitting football caps, scarves with the school crest and funky socks should appeal to the pupils. Making learning fun encourages participation and interest.

## Your interest in this post

Please state why you are applying for this post and say what particular attributes, qualities or special areas of interest or expertise you would bring to it. (Use the continuation sheet if necessary.)

I am a very well-qualified and experienced teacher. My main subject of interest is silk screen printing, in which I have been specializing for the last 10 years. My background at the Thames College of Art and as an illustrator has enabled me to develop my own work using a silk screen mono print technique which is innovative and allows for great creative flexibility. I learned valuable technical skills from my first job in a printing company after leaving school. In my last job I was able to teach screen printed textiles very successfully to all GCSE groups. Results were good and the course was always popular.

Creativity cannot flourish in a chaotic environment, it grows from a basis of structured resources from which disciplined work can take place. I take great pride in being a very well-organized person who is a hard-working and conscientious team member. I enjoy using computers as a tool for administration and planning and use them increasingly in my creative work. Pupils are confident and relaxed about using graphics packages and new technology is bound to become a mainstay of art and design work in the future.

I have a genuine enthusiasm for my subject and a talent for teaching. There is no greater motivation than inspiring and educating young people. I love to use my skills and experience to stimulate creativity and enjoy helping to open up the world of artistic thinking to them. I am good humoured and patient, even under pressure. Children learn and work at different speeds and in different ways and respond best to a tolerant and supportive teacher who has high expectations.

I teach in a focused and firm manner, always trying to raise standards, but I am also a good listener with a calm understanding of some of the difficulties that students can face. Many ex-pupils have remained in contact with me over the years, saying that appreciation of the many facets of the art world has made a great impact on them and enhanced their lives.

In version B, the candidate has expanded on her application much more. You can see that if both versions were in a pile of application forms, version A would look dull and limited compared with version B. It is always a good idea to give more information, explain yourself and offer a deeper view of your motivation to provide a more rounded picture of yourself. In this way, employers can see what you are like and are more likely to invite you to an interview.

Holding back is the wrong tactic when you are applying for jobs. You need to expand, embellish and explain, to come over with impact compared with other candidates. We all feel nervous about blowing our own trumpet. We worry that we will sound boastful or big-headed, but you can see from the example above that overcoming your natural modesty will not sound inappropriate. On the contrary, it will give you a big advantage in the job stakes. Saying the minimum is just not good enough. You need to really go to town with a winning picture of yourself. You are in competition with every other applicant in the pile on the employer's desk – so give your application everything you've got.

## Keeping records

When you have applied for a job, keep a copy of the application that you have sent off. If it is electronic, print it. You can file it along with the original advert and any paperwork sent to you by the company about the job. A ring-binder or wallet-style folder is ideal for this. Date your copy of the application form so that you know when you sent it off. A copy should always be saved on your computer too if you applied online and the copy you have printed should be kept, in case you lose the data.

You will need this copy if you are invited for an interview, so you can remember what you said about yourself. Even if this particular application goes no further, you may still be able to update and adapt what you have written for a future application for a similar position elsewhere.

## Follow-up

Some employers inform you as part of the job details they send out that unsuccessful applicants will not be notified, but otherwise they should let you know the outcome of your application. The reason that sometimes no notification is sent is that sending out many letters costs a lot of money. You will still know if you have been successful or not by whether or not you receive an invitation to the next stage of the selection process.

If you do not hear from the employer and you are expecting a reply, you can always ring up or e-mail the organization to find out what has happened to your application. Make sure that you allow a realistic period for the employer to process the applications and always be polite and courteous when you call or write.

You will of course feel edgy and keyed-up if you ring, but the tone and type of words you use can make the difference between creating a good impression and alienating the person on the other end of the line. Candidates who sound hostile about the progress of their applications can make employers feel worried about the threat of legal action on the grounds of discrimination. You are much more likely to get helpful and honest feedback if you sound open and positive when you make your enquiry. Make sure you choose your words carefully.

Don't say:

> 'I applied for that factory job. Why haven't I heard from you yet?'

This sounds aggressive and is likely to antagonise whoever picks up the telephone. A better approach would be:

> 'I wonder if you can help me? I recently sent in an application to work in your company and would like to ask if there is any news about an interview shortlist yet.'

Application forms do go astray sometimes, so checking on your progress in this way will at least ensure that your form has been properly considered and dealt with.

Employers and managers know that applicants are eager to get an interview and will try to be helpful if you sound pleasant and friendly. Similarly, if you are not offered an interview, you could contact the company to try to get some hints about why you were unsuccessful. This depends on your nerve, but a suggested formula could be:

> 'Thank you for informing me that I have not been successful in my job application. Would it be possible for someone to give me some brief ideas about improving my approach to future vacancies? I would be very grateful for any help that you can offer.'

This may well encourage a full and positive response which could ensure your success next time around, rather than you getting a cagey, non-committal brush-off. The employer will be doing you a favour if he or she does give you feedback of this kind, so make sure you give proper thanks. 'This is exactly the kind of work I am looking for, so your comments have been really useful. Thank you very much for your time', is one polite way of responding.

## Points to remember

1. You want the employer to feel that everything in your life so far has been leading up to this point, and that there is no better person for the job than you.

2. Try to use every question that is on the form to sell yourself to the employer.

3. Spend time thinking about the key areas of work in the job, then establish the skills and experience you have that give you the edge.

4. Treat all the sections of the form as equally important. Mess up the early questions and an employer may not bother reading any further.

## Dos and don'ts

✔ Do read the form through carefully first and then follow all the instructions. Plan your answers before you write anything.

✔ Do write out your application in rough first. The more care you take over the task, the better your chances of success.

✔ Do stress your good points. Let the employer know that he or she would be lucky to have you as an employee.

✔ Do make clear and concise points when you write. Waffle is not impressive but personal examples to back up your claims will do the trick.

✔ Do allow yourself plenty of time to complete the form, particularly if you are posting it. A rushed application may lose you the job and copies sent by fax or e-mail at the last minute never create such a good impression. If you really have to fax or e-mail a form unexpectedly, make sure you ring the company first to check this is acceptable. Then also send the form by post afterwards.

✗ Don't tell lies. You could lose your job if you are found out.

✗ Don't scribble out mistakes. Use correction fluid or put one neat line through the material concerned using a ruler.

✗ Don't send in your CV with an application form unless you are asked to do so.

✗ Don't miss out any questions. Check the completed form thoroughly before you send it off. Boxes left blank can give an impression of offhandedness.

Remember to sign and date the form if asked to do so. Many people leave this to the end and then forget to actually do it.

✗ Don't send in your form after the closing date. It is unlikely to be considered unless you have gained the employer's permission in advance to do this.

# 7

# Letters of application

Sometimes job advertisements ask you to send in your CV together with a letter of application. Read *Preparing the Perfect CV* (published by Kogan Page) to find out how to put together a CV of which you can be proud. Sending a CV to a company with no letter of explanation is confusing, so you need to write a bold, confident and clear letter to accompany it. The letter should be addressed to the named person if you are replying to an advertisement, and it is often helpful to say where you saw the vacancy advertised.

If you are sending the letter as a speculative approach, just to see if the organization has any vacancies, try to find out the name of the right person to contact and address the letter to him or her personally.

The letter needs to explain the following:

- why you are sending your CV;
- significant things about your background and skills;
- the sort of person you are;
- the special contribution you can offer;
- what you would like to happen next;
- how you can be contacted.

Everyone who applies for jobs in this way sends in a dynamic letter with their CV, so yours must be strong in order to compete. The letter cannot just be a brief note to say why the CV has arrived; it must be the selling point of the application. CVs do not stand alone they can be useful, but as a back-up to a powerful introductory letter. As well as details about you and your background, this letter gives you the chance to explain what extra value you can bring to the organization. This may mean explaining your 'vision' for the position you are applying for – how you would approach the job. Do not make the letter longer than two sides, and the tone should be courteous and detailed. Do not worry about repeating information contained in your CV. The letter may well be separated from the CV and, in any case, it does no harm to re-state your good points.

You should use good quality paper. Remember that, however neat your writing, it is not the same as the employer's and is therefore not nearly as easy to read as typed script. Prove this for yourself by seeing how much faster it is to read newsprint than a letter from someone you do not know. If there is no way you can get access to a method of typing your letter, then work hard to ensure your writing is exceptionally neat, even and clear.

## Examples

The following pages contain eight examples of letters of application for people in different situations. One or more of them may be relevant to you, as you consider how to compose your own letters to employers.

These examples are included to give you an idea of the many different ways in which such letters can be written. Although the names and addresses are fictitious, all the details come from letters written by successful job-seekers. No letter will be appropriate for every situation, but the examples have been chosen to represent a range of circumstances. Do not copy these letters, but see if they give you ideas for approaches of your own.

# 1 Speculative approach

Maria MacDonald
Basement Flat, 2 Arbour Fields
Richmond
N Yorks. YO1 3PJ
mmac@corfield.com


Date …

Mr David Belton, Director
Salcott Equipment
33 Pinks Lane
Richmond
N Yorks. YO4 2LG

Dear Mr Belton

I am writing to enquire if you have any vacancies in your company. I enclose my CV for your information. As you can see, I have spent ten years working with a variety of different machinery and equipment and am used to industrial work.

I am a steady and serious person who works hard and fits easily into a new team. I am clean and careful in my work and can lend a hand in the office when needed. I am quick to pick up new instructions and flexible about the hours that I work. It was normal for me to do shift-work in my last job. I am known for taking a pride in my work and want to work for a company with a reputation for producing quality goods – hence my application to Salcott's.

I have excellent references and would be delighted to discuss any possible vacancy with you at your convenience. In case you do not have any suitable openings at the moment, I would be grateful if you would keep my CV on file for any future possibilities.

Thank you for your attention to this matter. I look forward to hearing from you.

Yours sincerely


Maria MacDonald

Enc:

## 2 College leaver

Adrian Miller
97 Potter's Close
Sedgefield
Teesside
RT3 3PP
aam@corfield.com

Date ...

Ms Louise Powell
Powell's Energy Company
200 Seymour Industrial Estate
Hartfield Road
Middlesbrough GT99 1LZ

Dear Ms Powell

Please find enclosed my CV in application for the post advertised in *The Guardian* on 20 October.

The nature of my degree course has prepared me for this position. The course involved a great deal of independent research, relying on a substantial amount of translating into French and Spanish. I also studied economic history and for one course (History of Latin America since Independence) an understanding of the petro-chemical industry was essential. I found this subject very stimulating.

I am a fast and accurate writer, with a keen eye for detail and I should be very grateful for the opportunity to progress to market reporting.

I have not only the ability to take on the responsibility of this position immediately, but I believe that I also have the enthusiasm and determination to ensure that I make a success of it.

Thank you for taking the time to consider this application and I look forward to hearing from you in the near future.

Yours sincerely


Adrian Miller

Enc:

## 3   Woman returner

Sherena Williams
Hazelwood Cottage
Sway
Hampshire, SO42 6PY
sher@corfield.com

Date ...

The Personnel Manager
Hall's Ltd
100 London Road
Brockenhurst
Hampshire, SO14 1LS

Dear Sir/Madam

Re: Accounts Manager Vacancy

I am writing in reply to your advertisement in this week's *Hampshire Times*. I enclose my CV for your information. As you can see, I trained in accounting at Bishop's Technical College, gaining a BTEC pass. For ten years I ran the accounts department of Nicholson's Bakery in Lymington. I covered the whole variety of work in this busy office, from handling petty cash and making wage payments to credit control. I regularly used computerized accounts packages.

I left this post in 2004 to bring up my two young children. Being a full-time parent has enabled me to acquire new skills, such as scheduling and keeping to deadlines, organizing, communicating on different levels, delegating work and using my creative imagination to solve problems.

I am patient and flexible, stay calm in difficult situations, and am confident when working with figures and running an office. I am hard-working and thorough and am looking forward to resuming my career with a pace-making organization like Hall's.

I would be happy to discuss this application in more detail and look forward to hearing from you.

Yours faithfully

Sherena Williams

Enc:

# 4 School/College leaver

---

Fola Okintola
111 Poulton Terrace
Sidcup
Kent. DA14 6PZ
fola@corfield.com

Date ...

The Personnel Director
Haddleston Council
Haddleston
Kent, ST1 5AG

Dear Sir/Madam

Re: Vacancies for Junior Trainees

I would like to apply for the vacancy for junior trainee which I saw in my local Connexions office.

I left Cole Comprehensive School this year after taking my GCSE exams. I passed in English, Mathematics and General Science and won a prize for a project on 'Science and Ecology' earlier in my final year. I enclose a copy of my CV and my Record of Achievement which shows my progress throughout the last two years.

I am good at bringing the best out of other people and enjoyed in my sports lessons at school, being a key player in the volleyball team. I have worked each summer for the last three years as an assistant in the local sports centre helping to organize the summer sports programme which the Council runs each year for school children.

I am interested in working for the Council because I believe that local services are important. I take a pride in living in this area and know that your recent Quality Initiative has made people realize how much they depend on good street lighting and cleaning, housing and leisure facilities.

I would like to become a part of the team of people that organizes such services and look forward to discussing how I can contribute to the work of the Council in due course.

Thank you for your time. I look forward to hearing from you.

Yours faithfully

Fola Okintola
Enc:

# 5  Mature candidate

Louis Coombe
80 Bryan Ridge
Westminster Parade
London SW15 0LT
lc@corfield.com

Date ...

Mrs Alberga
Personnel Manager
Kogan and Company
Norman Street
London W1 4TK

Dear Mrs Alberga

Re: Adviser, Training Unit

Please find enclosed my CV. I have had many years' successful experience as a personnel manager in the clothing industry. Working with teams of different people meant that I quickly became adaptable and flexible.

I am at present updating my computer skills at a local resource centre and I have been helping the tutors there, on a voluntary basis, with the new trainees. I introduce them to the centre and act as a mentor during their training programme.

I devote time to making sure that everyone works well together and can recognize problems before they become insurmountable. I am approachable and tolerant but maintain high standards and communicate quickly and clearly with others. I am known for my ability to make learning fun and can always motivate people to give more of themselves. My mature outlook allows me to be a soothing influence at difficult times and I have a wide experience of work to draw on when needed.

I would enjoy contributing to the training provided by your company as I know of your excellent reputation in this field. I have a relative who works in your Northern Region who tells me that your staff development programme is very effective at building and motivating the team.

I would be delighted to discuss any detail of my application at your convenience. Thank you for your attention to this matter. I look forward to hearing from you.

Yours sincerely

Louis Coombe

Enc:

## 6 Made redundant

Debbie Cook
48 Half Moon Lane
Cardiff
CF4 3MN

Date ...

J Roberts
Whitefriars
Orion Street
Cardiff
CF3 8JJ

Dear Mr Roberts

Re: Sales Assistant Vacancy

Please find my CV enclosed for the vacancy for a Sales Assistant as advertised in *The Evening Post* of 12 October 2009.

I have had a lot of experience in the retail sector. I worked in different shops in Cardiff until I started work at Cordworths in 2000. I was there until earlier this year when the company was closed.

I enjoyed the work, took a pride in helping customers, ordering the stock and maintaining a tidy environment. Customers loved our branch and many of them were regulars. I was a key member of the group of staff, and I helped to establish a friendly and supportive team atmosphere. Jobs in big shops can be very hard work sometimes and you need the team to be able to pull together to solve problems and keep everything working smoothly.

The managers relied on senior staff such as myself to help with induction of new staff by showing them the ropes and helping them settle in. Security was a big issue in Cordworths and I was responsible for stock checks and till reconciliations. My personality is well suited to shop work. I like serving people, am careful with stock and can be relied upon to work hard and put the company first.

I do hope I get the chance of an interview so I can tell you more about the contribution I could make to Whitefriars. I look forward to hearing from you.

Yours sincerely

Debbie Cook

Enc:

# 7   College leaver

Heather Hewitt
157 Fourways Street
Doncaster
DN4 2CX

Date ...

Mrs Charlesworth
Senior Administrator
Carleton Chambers
Doncaster
DN2 1WD

Dear Mrs Charlesworth

Re: Legal Secretary, trainee position

I am applying for the trainee Legal Secretary position in your chambers. It was advertised in my college careers office. Please find my CV attached.

I have just finished my legal secretary's course at Portmans College. I studied for two years and undertook two placements in different chambers during my studies. We covered all the main work of a legal secretary including safe and proper handling of documents, layout and proofing and fast, accurate word processing. The most important of these skills is accuracy. Without that, legal cases can fall, just because of paperwork deficiencies. I was proud to get a distinction in this part of the course.

I learned a lot from my work placements while at college. It was interesting to see how barristers work and I was allowed to attend court as an observer on two occasions. I could see that a high standard of preparation is needed to win cases.

I am looking to come to work for chambers where I can feel one of the team. I enjoy using my skills and am ambitious to become a mainstay of the department, where I can represent the firm with other companies and clients as well as keep up the level and quality of work behind the scenes.

I would love to expand more on the contribution that I could make at an interview. Thank you for your attention to this matter. I look forward to hearing from you in due course.

Yours sincerely

Heather Hewitt

Enc:

## 8   Job changer

Jonathon Talbot
15 Water Lane
Stainsbrook
Middx
ST3 4RT

Date ...

Mr Darwin
Smallweeds Garden Centre
Stainsbrook
Middx
ST1 0JM

Dear Sir

I am applying for the post of landscape gardener with your firm after seeing the advertisement in today's community newspaper. You can see from my CV that I worked for several years in telephone sales and did well in my career there. However, it was a tough job and the commission-only pay structure in my firm led to immense pressure and an uneven work–life balance.

Three years ago I retrained in landscape gardening to fulfil a long-held dream to begin a new career. My interest in plants and gardens started when I had my own small section of our garden, in which I grew vegetables. As a teenager, my parents asked me to look after the rest of the garden as I was so obsessed with making it look nice.

I thoroughly enjoyed my training course, particularly the aspects of plant knowledge and structural studies. I am unusual as I enjoy maintaining gardens just as much as I do designing them. This means that I don't get bored by regular routine tasks. I get as much satisfaction from clipping shrubs twice a year and sweeping up leaves as from creating a new green space to the requirements of clients.

I have been working locally whilst studying and my contacts all love my work. I believe in establishing great relationships with my clients and they always want me to come back again. The key to building up a successful business is customer satisfaction and I know that at Smallweeds you are well known for your high standards of customer care.

I would love to use my new skills and bring my enthusiasm and commitment to your landscape design team. Thank you, I look forward to meeting you at an interview.

Yours sincerely

Jonathan Talbot
Enc:

Notice how in each of these examples the candidates are trying to phrase their application in terms that will appeal to the employer. They have thought through:

■ what the job involves;

■ what they have to offer in skills and experience that can be transferred to the new position;

■ how their personalities will fit.

They have made sure that they convey this clearly and simply in their letters. They sound keen and enthusiastic without giving the impression that they are desperate. They give clear reasons for the employer to want to take their application further. Most important, they spend time demonstrating to the reader how they can contribute to the organization.

Notice also how they write the letter itself. They know that their letter must be easy to read and follow if they are to attract the employer's attention when he or she has a pile of other applications to consider. They write as if they were sitting and talking in front of the employer at an interview – clearly but politely. Good writing does not mean using the longest words and the most complicated sentences that you can think up. It means being concise and to the point, and keeping your sentences short.

None of the letters is gimmicky or flashy. All the writers believe that they have serious skills to offer and the right personality to fit into the environment concerned. Their letters convey that information to the employer in an impressive way. You can tell that each writer has spent time and trouble composing the letter in order to make sure that it hits the mark.

Each letter ends with a thank you and is correctly addressed and typed for easy reading.

## Letters with your application form

Some employers expect a brief letter to accompany the application form. These are the views of the Director of Communications for a health organization that regularly recruits office staff:

'Do send a covering letter but don't make it too long. It is not like sending a CV where the letter is part of the application but it still needs to be more than "Please find my application enclosed. I look forward to expanding on this at interview." I always read the covering letter as I find it helps me form a first impression and differentiates between the different applications I am seeing. I expect you to give me one paragraph about why you are great for the job and why you would like to come and work for me. Those who add one more paragraph saying what they would do in the job stand an even better chance.'

### Points to remember

1. Letters of application can echo the key points from your application or CV, but should state your reasons for applying in different words.

2. You can use a letter to bring out factors that are specially relevant to the post, particularly if you are sending it with an application form where your answers may have been more constrained by the questions on the form.

3. Tailor and rewrite each letter for the specific job you are applying for. Cutting and pasting big chunks of typing from previous applications looks clumsy and will not impress.

## Dos and don'ts

✔ Do limit the letter to only two sides of A4 at most.

✔ Do give examples of the claims you are making for yourself.

✔ Do keep sentences short and punchy if you want the letter to be read.

✘ Don't talk about why you want the job: the employer is only interested in what you have to offer.

✘ Don't sound dull: use enthusiastic language to show you are keen.

✘ Don't close any doors. Try to get your letter and CV kept on file if there are no current vacancies.

# 8

# How to get that job!

## Case studies

All the characters in the following case studies had some difficulty with their application forms. Read their stories, which illustrate what can go wrong, see the comments from real employers and understand how the job-seekers could improve their techniques.

## Wayne

Wayne was quite good at filling in application forms and was always keen to do his extensive experience justice. He had some trouble fitting in details of all his varied jobs in the 'Previous Experience' space provided, despite keeping his writing small and neat. He added an extra piece of paper to ensure that everything he had ever done was included.

The employer said:

'It is ridiculous to cram in so much tiny writing in order to get all his jobs included. It put me off trying to read through it, especially as a lot of his previous jobs had nothing in common with the post I am trying to fill. He would have done himself more favours if he had just highlighted those jobs that were particularly relevant to this position. He could then have indicated that he also had other experience to offer, but just summarized what that was rather than listing each position. The whole experience was depressing, as an otherwise good candidate made himself appear a bad judge of how to present himself on the form.'

Wayne's eagerness to be honest about his background made him list every single job that he had ever had. Although the question asked about his previous experience it did not mean that he had to include details about absolutely every place he had ever worked.

Bullet points of those that were relevant to the position applied for, either because they were similar companies or because he had been involved with similar work, would have saved space. A sentence at the end saying that he had 'had additional experience in other areas of employment and could give further details if required' would have covered the rest of his working history perfectly adequately. A more confident approach of this sort would have helped his application.

## Mark

Mark prided himself on having excellent writing skills. He dashed off his applications with a flourish and was confident that the content of his forms was always excellent. He had worked in senior positions in the past and knew he had a lot to offer. He never bothered to do a rough copy first because he was an experienced job applicant and felt it would just be a waste of his time.

The employer said:

'Mark's form was just messy. He could have been quite an impressive candidate but the application looks as though he had taken no time over its completion. The way he presented himself put me off spending any more time on this form. Candidates have to understand that with many, many forms (sometimes up to 100) in front of me, I am not going to bother digging out nuggets. Unless everything about an application is impressive, it goes on the reject pile, I'm afraid.'

Being tidy makes a huge difference. In the same way as you try to dress up smartly and impressively for a job interview, you need to present yourself well at the paper stage. We can see from this example that even a well-qualified, experienced senior candidate can let himself down by not taking time and trouble over the way he fills forms in. You can be known for your skills and knowledge in your present job, but when you apply for a new position somewhere else, they will judge your ability from your application alone. Most jobs require presentation skills, either in written communications or in person. You will be judged on this, not only by what you say about yourself on the form but also on the impact your form makes compared with the others in the pile. You can help your chances of being called for an interview by ensuring that your application is consistently neat and well presented.

## Leila

Leila really wanted the job and her employer had asked her to put in for the promotion position. She was thrilled to have been encouraged to apply, and gave herself several weeks to fill the form in. Every evening after work she sat down and tried to complete it, but found she just could not get started. She got more and more worried as the deadline approached and there was still nothing written on her rough copy. The last night she rushed to fill in the form, but by the time it was finished, she was so disappointed in the way it looked, she tore it up and put it in the bin.

The employer said:

'We were so keen for Leila to apply for the job and had specifically suggested to her that she did so. For some reason she missed the deadline and did not put an application in at all. For the lack of that one form, she missed her chance for a significant promotion and seven thousand pounds more a year. To be honest, a terribly presented form that just listed her present responsibilities would have got her an interview, because the promotion was right up her street. Without the application form there was nothing we could do but give the job to the next best candidate.'

Leila really shot herself in the foot here. Her confidence let her down to the extent that she could not even fill in the form well enough to hand it in. As her employer said, had she given in almost anything, she would have probably got an interview, but without any kind of formal expression of interest from her, her employer could not proceed with her as a candidate. It is such a shame as she herself was the only thing holding her back. She was her own worst enemy. She really needed to just knuckle down to the task as if it were like filling in a form for work.

Had she just made a start in the early stages, she would have been able to get the form finished and handed in. The longer she left it though, the more difficult the task seemed to be. In fact all she had to do was describe her current duties and her educational background – not too difficult to do when looked at rationally. If you find yourself stuck in a similar way, break the difficult tasks down into small parts. Start by filling in the factual details about yourself, go on to the education and employment history, then finish with why you would be suitable for the job. You will find that by concentrating on only one part at a time the whole task is much more painlessly completed.

## Victoria

Victoria tried very hard with her application form. She felt she would be good at the job concerned but she was also worried about how to sell herself on paper. She spent weeks fretting over the form, asking friends to comment on what she had written and rewriting it several times. She was concerned that she show herself to be an honest person who did not make any claims about her abilities that could not be substantiated.

The employer said:

> 'This form was just boring compared to all the others I saw. She seemed to not really want the job. Most applicants come over as keen to state their strong points, but Victoria was so low-key that it was hard to find any particular contribution that she thought she could make. Application forms have to work extra hard to make the candidate sound dynamic and significant, otherwise we have no reason to invite them to come and tell us more at interview.'

It is possible to be too honest on an application form. Victoria was so keen not to over-sell herself that she ended up doing just the opposite and leaving the recruiter stone cold in response. Everyone talks up their strengths and describes themselves at their very best when filling in forms. This is not the way that nice people usually put themselves across to other people. The nicer you are in fact, the more modest and self-effacing you are likely to be in real life. But the qualities that we admire in a friend just do not work well when trying to get an interview.

You need to exaggerate your good qualities and boost up your skills and strengths when the only medium through which you can express yourself is a paper application. If Victoria had been given a six-month trial in the job, the employer could well have been convinced that she was the woman for the post. However, her abilities had to jump off the page compared with those of other people in order for her to be in with a chance. Our aim is to create a paper representation of ourselves from what we put on the form, otherwise all that is there is a two-dimensional list of what we have done and where we have been.

Victoria should have put her natural reticence to one side and made the most of every good thing about herself. With positive dynamic language and vivid examples of her strengths, the contribution she could make in the job would have become suddenly visible.

## Stephen

Stephen knew he could do the job on offer. He had not long left college and the vacancy was perfect for his skills and personality. The trouble was that he did not have any very relevant experience. He filled in the form as best he could, stating his claim that he would be very good in the position and was keen to get to the interview stage so that he could impress them with his character and outlook.

The employer said:

'Unfortunately we could not take the risk of bringing Stephen in to the interview phase of this recruitment exercise. He may have been a great candidate but he did not make a good enough case for his inclusion on his application form. Without any relevant experience since college, we had nothing to go on to take this application further. He said he thought he would be good but gave no examples to illustrate why this was the case. If he had made some links with college activities to the work we do, or if he could have shown how he had picked up his understanding of our work, it may have been different. If your form does not shout loudly that you should be kept in, then you will be out. A bit more thought about how much needs to go in to the form could have saved the day.'

Stephen's confidence in person had not translated onto his application form. You cannot expect employers to be able to see into a crystal ball and just 'know' that you could do the job. You have to make the case yourself, and if there is any particular reason they might not pick you for interview, you have to work doubly hard to counter this. Stephen knew that his lack of relevant experience represented a major gap between what the employer was looking for and his own background.

There is a fine line between highlighting any bit of experience that you can reasonably claim will give you transferable skills for a job and making spurious claims to have experience when you have not. In Stephen's case he could perhaps have made more of what he had done at college or since he left. He could have compensated a little for his lack of directly relevant experience had he projected himself into the job and described how he would work if given the position. However, if the job had asked for three years' relevant experience of working in teams and on projects, then perhaps he would be wise to find a way of getting that kind of experience before applying for such a job. Perhaps a different post as a stepping stone to applying for this one later on, or some voluntary experience where he could build up his years of valuable experience, could get him where he wants to be in the longer term.

## Points to remember

1. Even the most employable and brilliant candidates get rejected sometimes, so do not let a disappointment get you down.

2. Application forms can seem the least exciting part of the recruitment process, but they represent the gateway to the all-important interview.

3. Completing an application form you feel proud of can be an excellent rehearsal for meeting the employer in person later on.

4. Without this time to think through why you would make a good contribution to the post, you would be unconfident at the interview.

5. You know if the employer takes your application further that you stand as good a chance as the other shortlisted candidates.

## Dos and don'ts

✔ Do change your approach if you keep getting rejected at the application stage.

✔ Do involve other people you trust in your efforts: sometimes a different point of view can help you complete the more difficult questions when you get stuck.

✔ Do keep the rest of your life going while you are applying for jobs: you need to remain a well-rounded person, not turn into a job search bore.

✗ Don't tell the world about every job you apply for – it can be embarrassing if you don't get anywhere.

✗ Don't get overwhelmed by the task ahead: everyone has to complete application forms and we all find it difficult sometimes.

✗ Don't give up. If you keep making applications and keep trying to improve you will get there one day soon.

# Application form blanks

You may find these six blank forms useful to practise on, even if there is no particular job vacancy that you are interested in at the moment.

**1**

| APPLICATION FORM EDUCATION | |
|---|---|
| Academic Qualifications (please give subjects) | Professional Qualifications (please give dates) |
| | |

| TRAINING COURSES | | |
|---|---|---|
| Organizing Body | Title of Course | Dates Attended |
| | | |

Are you a car owner?    Yes/No
Do you hold a valid driving licence?    Yes/No

## EMPLOYMENT HISTORY

| Employer (current or most recent first) | Job title and brief description of duties | Grade | Salary | Dates employed | Reason for leaving |
|---|---|---|---|---|---|
| | | | | | |

## ADDITIONAL INFORMATION

Please give the following information:

(A)  The reasons why you are applying for this post.
(B)  Any experience you may have which is related to this post.

## INTERESTS AND ACTIVITIES

Briefly outline your hobbies and interests

Please give the names and addresses of two referees:
(ONE MUST BE YOUR PRESENT EMPLOYER)

NAME ...............................................  NAME ...............................................

POSITION ......................................  POSITION ......................................

ADDRESS ......................................  ADDRESS ......................................

................................................................  ................................................................

................................................................  ................................................................

................................................................  ................................................................

POSTCODE ...................................  POSTCODE ...................................

MAY WE CONTACT PRIOR TO
INTERVIEW?

YES/NO

MAY WE CONTACT PRIOR TO
INTERVIEW?

YES/NO

NOTICE PERIOD REQUIRED?

IF SELECTED FOR INTERVIEW WOULD YOU BE AVAILABLE ON

...........................................?

YES/NO

I confirm that to the best of my knowledge the information given on this form
is true and can be treated as any subsequent Contract of Employment.

Date ...................................................  Signature ...........................................

**2**

APPLICATION FORM

For Office Use

APPLICATION FOR THE POST OF _____

PERSONAL DETAILS

FORENAME(S) _____ SURNAME _____

ADDRESS _____

_____

(INCLUDING POST CODE) _____

DATE OF BIRTH _____ SEX: MALE/FEMALE
(Not always compulsory)

TELEPHONE: HOME _____ DAYTIME _____

CURRENT DRIVING LICENCE: YES/NO    CAR OWNER: YES/NO

------------------------------------------------------------------

Do you have any special requirements to enable you to attend for interview, eg access, interpreters? Please indicate below.

## DETAILS OF EDUCATION, TRAINING AND QUALIFICATIONS

| Dates Attended | Full-time or Part-time | Name and Town of Secondary School/College/ University | Qualifications/ Examinations – state subjects & examining board | Date Gained |
|---|---|---|---|---|
| | | | | |
| | | | | |
| | | | | |

## REFERENCES

Two persons to whom approach may be made should be listed. If you do not wish any reference to be sought at this stage, please place an X in the relevant box.

Name:                                         Name:

☐   Full Address:                 ☐   Full Address:

Telephone No:                         Telephone No:

PLEASE INDICATE YOUR REASONS FOR SEEKING THIS POST, HIGHLIGHTING ANY PERSONAL SKILLS WHICH YOU BELIEVE WOULD BE OF PARTICUALR RELEVANCE OR VALUE.

## PAST EMPLOYMENT   (Please include part-time or holiday jobs)

Employer:                                 Type of Work/Responsibilities

## VOLUNTARY WORK EXPERIENCE   (For example, involvement in community fundraising, play group, committee work.)

## PRESENT EMPLOYMENT   (if applicable)

Employer's Name            ..................................................................
and Address                ..................................................................
                           ..................................................................
Date Started               ..................................................................
Type of Work/Responsibilities:

## 3

# Confidential application form

Position applied for

How did you hear of the vacancy?

Surname (Mr/Mrs/Ms/Miss)           (BLOCK LETTERS PLEASE)
                                    Address

Forenames

Telephone No. (Home)               (Work)

Nationality

Are you prepared to move house –    What locations in England and Wales
                                    would be most and least acceptable to
                                    you?

For this position                  Most acceptable

For future promotion               Least acceptable

Do you have a full driving licence?   YES/NO

To assist us in monitoring our policy of equal opportunities, we would be grateful if
you could tick the appropriate box.
I would describe my ethnic origin as
  African    Afro-Caribbean    Asian    European–UK    European–other    Other –
                                                                         please specify

  ☐          ☐                 ☐        ☐               ☐                 ☐

## School Record (after age 11)

| Name & address of School/College | Dates From | To | Educational Qualifications (specify all subjects and attempts) | | | | | |
|---|---|---|---|---|---|---|---|---|
| | | | GCSEs or equivalent | | | | | |
| | | | Subject | Grade | Date | Subject | Grade | Date |
| | | | 'A' levels or equivalent | | | | | |
| | | | Subject | Grade | Date | Subject | Grade | Date |

## Further Education Record

| Name of Universities/Colleges attended (f/t or p/t) plus dates | Subjects taken | BSc, BA etc | Qualification Level/Class expected or obtained | Date obtained |
|---|---|---|---|---|
| | | | | |

## Professional Qualifications

| Give the dates and results of all professional examinations taken (including intermediate stages) | Results | Dates |
|---|---|---|
| | | |

# Employment History

Please give details of your present or most recent job

From                                    Main duties and responsibilities

To

Name and address of employer

                                        Main achievements

Nature of business

Job title                               Organization chart indicating your main position

Starting salary

Most recent salary

Reason for leaving


Please give details of your second most recent job

From                                    Main duties and responsibilities

To

Name and address of employer

                                        Main achievements

Nature of business

Job title                               Organization chart indicating your main position

Starting salary

Most recent salary

Reason for leaving

Please list any job before those mentioned overleaf

| From | To | Name of employer | Job title | Salary | |
|------|----|-----------------|-----------|--------|--------|
| | | | | Start | Finish |

## Interests/Responsibilities
What are your main interests/responsibilities outside work?

## Career Plans
Describe briefly the development of your career to date, your plans for the future and the attraction of this job.

Are there any particular questions you would like to raise at interview?

Any further information you may care to give which may be relevant to your application.

## Referees

Please give the name, address and position of two referees who can comment on your work performance. At least one of these should be connected with your present (or most recent) place of employment or study.

1.                                                    2.

Position                                     Position

Please give the name, address and occupation of one referee unconnected with employment who has known you for at least three years to whom reference may be made.

Occupation

Have you been convicted of any criminal offences which are not yet 'spent' under the Rehabilitation of Offenders Act 1974?
(Please give details or answer 'No')

Please give details of any major illness and/or any chronic conditions/allergies.

Please give details of any time lost from work/full-time education in the last five years through ill health or other incapacity.

Are you registered disabled?    YES/NO

How much notice are you required to give?

Signature                                   Date

Note:    a) It will be accepted that we may approach your past employers (BUT NOT YOUR PRESENT EMPLOYER), unless you make a note to the contrary below, showing the organization we may not approach without prior permission.
    b) Any false or misleading statements made on this form may, if they subsequently come to light, be taken to justify dismissal from employment with the Commission or could result in the cancellation of any job offer made.

## 4

## *APPLICATION FOR EMPLOYMENT*
## *STRICTLY CONFIDENTIAL*

**Please complete in black or blue ink or type**

| Application for position of: | Advert reference number: |
|---|---|
| Surname (block capitals): | Other name(s): |

| Address:<br><br><br>Postcode: | |
|---|---|

| Telephone (Home):<br><br>Telephone (Mobile): | Telephone (Work):<br><br>*Leave blank if you do not wish it used* |
|---|---|
| E-mail address: | Are you related to any member of the company's council or to any employee of the company?     YES/NO |

| Pharmacist/Technician Registration Number (if applicable):<br>*(delete where appropriate)* | |
|---|---|
| Nationality: | Are you required to hold a work permit? YES/NO |

*If the posiiton involves travelling:* Do you hold a current driving licence?    YES/NO
If yes, do you have any current endorsements? *Please give appropriate details.*

# EMPLOYMENT HISTORY

## Present or most recent employment

| Name and address of employer and type of business: | | | |
|---|---|---|---|
| Position held: | From:           To: | | Salary (including any commission or bonus). |
| Reason for leaving/wishing to leave current post: | | | Notice required: |

## Previous employment

*Please enter in chronological order, most recent first.*

| Employer | Dates of employment From      To | Position held/ main responsibilities | Salary/reason for leaving |
|---|---|---|---|
| | | | |

Please write a brief description of your present duties and responsibilities.

**Skills, knowledge and experience**
*Please state below the reasons why you wish to apply for the position and what individual skills, knowledge and experience relevant to the post you have to offer. Include any other information, including leisure interests and activities, that you wish to add.*

Continue on a separate sheet if necessary.

# EDUCATION

**Education and qualifications (including membership of professional bodies)**

| Schools/Colleges/ Universities, etc | Dates: From          To | Examinations passed (including grades), Qualifications obtained |
|---|---|---|
| | | |

# TRAINING AND SHORT COURSES

*Please detail any recent training you have undertaken relevant to this post.*

*Please state number of days' absence because of sickness in the past 12 months and give reasons.*

# REFERENCES

Please give the names of two people, one of whom should be your present/most recent employer:

*References may be taken up for shortlisted candidates prior to interview. May we contact your present employer prior to interview?* **YES/NO**

| |
|---|
| Present/most recent employer:<br>Name:<br>Title:<br>In what capacity are you known to this person?<br><br>Address:<br><br><br><br><br><br>Postcode:<br>Telephone number: |
| Other referee:<br>Name:<br>Title:<br>In what capacity are you known to this person?<br><br>Address:<br><br><br><br><br>Postcode:<br>Telephone number: |

# Declaration

*I certifiy that to the best of my knowledge, the information provided on this application is correct. If, after appointment, the information given proves to be inaccurate, I accept that this would render me liable to disciplinary action under the appropriate procedure.*

*Signature:* _____

*Date:* _____

**Please note that the personal data provided on this form will be handled, processed and stored for recruitment and selection purposes.**

# 5

## JOB APPLICATION FORM

Please return completed applications to: HR Customer Service Team Glasgow

*PLEASE READ THE ENCLOSED GUIDANCE NOTES BEFORE COMPLETING THIS FORM*
**Complete in black ink**

| Job Title | Post Number |
|---|---|
| Directorate | Location |

## Personal details

| | |
|---|---|
| Title *(Mr, Mrs, Ms)* | |
| Forenames | National Insurance No |
| Last Name | Home Tel |
| Address | Mobile Tel |
| | Work Tel |
| Town | E-mail |
| County        Postcode | |

Are you an existing employee of this organization?          Yes          No

Do you have a disability/long-term illness?          Yes          No
(See Guidance Notes for definition)

If 'yes', indicate here if you are aware of any adjustments that the organization could make to help you apply for or carry out the job (see Guidance Notes)

Are you applying to do this job on job-sharing basis? Yes      If possible      No
*(for jobs over 30 hours per week only)*

# Education Qualifications

## You may be asked to provide evidence of qualifications obtained

| SECONDARY EDUCATION (CSE, GCE, GCSE, RSA, A Levels, etc) | | | | |
|---|---|---|---|---|
| Examination | Level | Subject(s) | Grade | Date of Exam |
| | | | | |
| | | | | |
| | | | | |

| FURTHER AND HIGHER EDUCATION (Degree, Diploma, BTEC, City & Guilds, NVQ, etc) | | | | | |
|---|---|---|---|---|---|
| Institution | Dates | Full or PT | Qualification | Subject | Pass Level or Grade |
| | | | | | |
| | | | | | |
| | | | | | |

## Qualifications and Training

## You may be asked to provide evidence of qualifications obtained

| Other relevant qualifications, including membership of professional bodies |
|---|
|  |

**Relevant training and personal development**
*(State who provided training, duration and dates)*
Examples could include: short courses, skills training, external awards/
activities, etc.

*continue on separate sheet if required*

# Current/latest employment

| Name and address of current/ most recent employer | Job title |
| --- | --- |
| | Current/latest salary and any benefits |
| | Weekly hours |
| Date started in post | Date of leaving *(if relevant)* |
| Notice required | Reason for leaving |

| Main duties/responsibilities/achievements |
| --- |
| |

# References

Normally, references will be requested for all candidates invited for interview, unless you ask us not to by ticking the 'no' box below. This will not affect our decision to invite you for interview. However, references will need to be taken up at some stage if you are successful. We operate a policy of open references. This means that you may read the reference, upon request.

Please give the names and addresses of two people who would be willing to supply a reference about you, including your most recent employer (or teacher/tutor, where appropriate), who have known you during the past three years, if that is possible. Please also state in what capacity they know you.

| Name | Name |
| --- | --- |
| Address | Address |
| Tel no | Tel no |
| E-mail address | E-mail address |
| Employer or Personal? | Employer or Personal? |
| Organization *(if applicable)* | Organization *(if applicable)* |

May we contact them if we decide to invite you for interview?

Yes        No

*(If 'no', we will contact you for permission before requesting references)*

**Canvassing of employees**
Canvassing of employees of the organization by you or on your behalf, is strictly forbidden and may invalidate your application.

**Indicate here if you are related to any employee of the organization, giving their name (and directorate, if known, where relevant).**
Please state **NONE** if appropriate.

**Entitlement to work in the UK**
To comply with the Asylum and Immigration Act 1996 all prospective employees will be asked to supply evidence of eligibility to work in the UK. We will ask to see an appropriate official document (for example, a document showing your National Insurance number, if you have one, your birth certificate, passport, etc.) **Do not send these now. Further information will be sent to you if you are selected.**

Do you require a work permit to work in the UK?        Yes        No
If you already have a work permit, please give the expiry date:

Do you have a current driving licence?        Yes        No
(Also see disability health section of the Guidance Notes)

**Please give licence details if job entails driving public service or heavy goods.**

**Give details of any penalties on your licence or convictions pending if driving is essential.**

## Work and other relevant experience

Please list below a complete record of other employments and activities, either paid or unpaid. These should be in date order, starting with the most recent.

| Dates from to | Name of organization and and nature or business | Job title/role with brief indication of main duties and responsibilities | Reason for leaving |
|---|---|---|---|
| | | | |
| | | | |
| | | | |
| | | | |

## How you meet the selection criteria

It is important that you provide evidence in this section of how you meet the essential and desirable criteria set out in the person specification. Tell us about things you were responsible for and what you achieved. Include examples from paid or unpaid work or other activities you have undertaken that are relevant to the job you are applying for. Also include other information about why you want the job and anything else you wish to say. **Please include headings linked to the criteria on the person specification.**

## Criminal Convictions

Please give details of criminal convictions below. Unless stated otherwise, you do not need to declare convictions which are 'spent', as defined by the Rehabilitation of Offenders Act 1974 and subsequent regulations.

However, if you are applying for a job supervising, caring for or otherwise connected with people from the following list, **you must always declare any convictions and/or cautions for criminal offences**, even where they are 'spent'. For these purposes, this includes working with children, young and older people, those who are dependent on alcohol or drugs, and those with mental or physical disabilities, illness or deformity, including people who are blind, deaf or without speech. For certain posts, police checks will be required. If it is necessary, you will be asked to sign a separate authorization.

| Details of criminal convictions   *Please state NONE if appropriate.* |
| --- |
| |

## Declaration

To the best of my knowledge, the information I have supplied on this form is correct. I understand that giving false information or omitting relevant information could disqualify my application and, if I am appointed, could lead to my dismissal. In submitting this form via e-mail I confirm the above to be true, and understand that I will be asked to sign this form if invited to interview.

In submitting this form I give my consent for personal data to be processed in accordance with the Data Protection Act 1988. I am aware that, for statistical purposes, my personal details may be shared with the organization's recruitment partners.

| Signed | Date |
| --- | --- |

**6**

## Application Form

Please complete all sections of this form in black ink or type. We do not shortlist candidates using CVs, therefore you must ensure that all applicable sections of this form are completed.

### Section 1: Personal Details

Position applied for:

Location/Service:

Job Reference:

Title:

First Name:

Surname:

Address:

Home Phone:

Work Phone:

Mobile Phone:

E-mail:

Please note that it may be necessary for us to contact you during office hours, though we will do so with the utmost discretion.

### Section 2: Education and Training

Please detail any academic or professional qualifications you currently hold or are working towards and professional memberships, starting with the most recent.

| Dates | School/College/Training Body | Qualification(s) |
| --- | --- | --- |
|  |  |  |
|  |  |  |
|  |  |  |
|  |  |  |

## Section 3: Employment History

**Current or most recent employer:**

| Employer: | Job title: |
|---|---|

| From/To (Month, Year): | Salary: |
|---|---|

| Notice Period: | Hours: |
|---|---|

Summary of Duties:

Reason for Leaving:

**Previous Employment:**

| Dates | Employer | Job Title and Duties |
|---|---|---|
| | | |
| | | |
| | | |
| | | |
| | | |

## Section 4: Supporting Your Application

Personal Statement:
Please refer to the role profile, which outlines skills, experience and knowledge required for this post. Please give details on how you meet these requirements. If you require more space, you may continue on a separate sheet, ensuring it is attached securely.

### References:
Please name two employment referees, who between them cover at least the last two years. If you have been unemployed, but in education, the names of your tutor and a referee from your last employer are necessary.

**Referee 1:**

Name (including title):

| Organization: | Job title: |
|---|---|
| Address: | Telephone Number: |
| | E-mail: |
| | Relationship: |
| Postcode: | May we contact them prior to interview? Yes/No |

**Referee 2:**

Name (including title):

| Organization: | Job title: |
|---|---|
| Address: | Telephone Number: |
| | E-mail: |
| | Relationship: |
| Postcode: | May we contact them prior to interview? Yes/No |

## Section 5: Other

If you answer 'Yes' to any of these questions, please include full details in the 'Additional Information' section on Page 5.

Are you related to any current or former employee, Board member or service user of ours? If yes please give brief details.

The post for which you are applying is exempt from the provisions of the Rehabilitation of Offenders Act 1974. It is a condition of employment that all unspent convictions and cautions are disclosed in the 'Additional Information' section. Failure to disclose such information could result in subsequent dismissal or disciplinary action.

Do you have any Criminal Convictions you need to disclose?　　　　Yes ☐　No ☐

Do you require a Work Permit?　　　　Yes ☐　No ☐

Do you hold a current UK Driving Licence?　　　　Yes ☐　No ☐

**Medical History:**

How many days have you been absent from work due to illness over the last 12 months?

Do you have any medical conditions that may have an impact on your ability to carry out this role?

If you have a disability, are there any specific facilities you require at an interview if shortlisted?

Would you describe yourself as having experienced personal problematic substance use?　　　　Yes ☐　No ☐

If you have replied 'yes' to the previous question:

Have you ever completed a rehabilitation course?　　　　Yes ☐　No ☐

Which service did you use?

When did you complete the programme?　　Date:

## Additional Information

Please use this space to supplement any answers to the questions in Section 5. If necessary, you may continue on another sheet of paper, ensuring all sheets are attached securely.

I confirm that the information is correct, even if submitted electronically without signature. I understand that false or misleading information or failure to disclose a conviction as defined above, may lead to dismissal. I also understand that the information may be entered into a computer and under the terms and conditions set out in the Data Protection Act will be treated in a secure and confidential manner.

| Signed: | Date: |
|---------|-------|

**Please return your completed form to:**

**J Thomas HR Department**

# Other sources of help

## Learn Direct Helpline

The Learn Direct Helpline, 0800 101 901, is funded by the government for everybody and gives free advice about local sources of help on careers and learning issues. This could include how to contact the organizations mentioned below. If you ask specifically where you can get help with job search skills, they will find out your most suitable local resource. Visit their comprehensive website for advice, help and information at www.learndirect.co.uk.

## The Connexions Service

Careers officers and personal advisers work with young people and sometimes adults to help them find the job or training of their choice. The understanding, skilled staff may be able to help you by checking over your form and they may provide access to a careers library where you can find information about different employers and jobs. Careers advisers will certainly be able to direct you to local resources for job-seekers. Find the number of your local Connexions Service and ring to find out more. Visit this excellent website for a huge database of free careers information at www.connexions-direct.com/jobs4u.

# Libraries

Libraries can be quiet places to complete application forms and the reference sections of main libraries have information about different companies and large employers, so you can find out about the main products and services and the company organization. Ask the librarian for help. Many libraries also have photocopiers for use by the public for a fee and can often provide internet access too.

# Jobcentre Plus

Government-funded jobcentres have skilled staff who can advise you on the best way to make applications. If you have been unemployed for a while you can use their job search facilities such as telephones, stationery, and sometimes computers to help you get a job. Contact your local Jobcentre Plus for details. Their website is at www.jobscentreplus.gov.uk.

# Careers Advice

This is a government-funded service offering free advice on courses, jobs and practical career issues. Call free on 0800 100 900 or visit www.careersadvice.direct.gov.uk

# Index